NELSON MANDELA

South Africa's Silent Voice of Protest

by Jim Hargrove

CHILDRENS PRESS®

CHICAGO

PICTURE ACKNOWLEDGMENTS

UPI/Bettmann Newsphotos—Frontispiece, 28,
55 (bottom right), 56 (bottom left and right), 57 (3 photos),
58 (top right and bottom), 59 (top), 120

AP/Wide World Photos—8, 16, 54 (2 photos), 55 (top and bottom left),
56 (top), 58 (top left), 59 (bottom), 60 (2 photos), 61 (2 photos), 62, 84, 96

Cover illustration by Len W. Meents

LIBRARY OF CONGRESS
Library of Congress Cataloging-in-Publication Data

Hargrove, Jim.
  Nelson Mandela : South Africa's silent voice of protest /
by Jim Hargrove.
    p. cm.
  Includes index.
  Summary: Presents the life and career of the
imprisoned leader of the African National Congress
focusing on his role in the struggle for black majority
rights in South Africa.
  ISBN 0-516-03266-6
  1. Mandela, Nelson, 1918-   —Juvenile literature.
2. Civil rights workers, South Africa—Biography—
Juvenile literature. 3. African National Congress—
Biography—Juvenile literature. 4. Anti-apartheid
movements—South Africa—Biography—Juvenile
literature. 5. Political prisoners—South Africa—Juvenile
literature. [1. Mandela, Nelson, 1918-   . 2. Civil rights
workers—South Africa. 3. Blacks—Biography.] I. Title.
DT779.95M36H36   1989
323.4'092'4—dc19
[B]   88-36746
                                              CIP
                                               AC

Table of Contents

Chapter 1

SOWETO

Early in 1988, an American reporter was completing a month-long visit to South Africa. He had spent much of his time in the city of Johannesburg, in the northern part of the country. Most reference books and other sources list either Johannesburg or Cape Town, depending on how residents are counted, as the largest city in South Africa.

But the American reporter knew that just ten miles southwest of Johannesburg is another city, larger than Cape Town, larger than Johannesburg, probably larger than both of them combined. The city is called Soweto. On most maps, Soweto is not even shown. With perhaps two million or more inhabitants, virtually all of them black Africans, Soweto is unquestionably the largest city in South Africa. It is denied the official honor, however, because it is not legally a city. The word Soweto stands for Southwest Townships, a collection of twenty-six different towns that looks to all the world like a single large city.

The American reporter, P. J. O'Rourke, talked to many of the white people who lived in and around Johannesburg. But none of them had ever been to Soweto, only ten miles away. None of them had even seen it.

On his last day in South Africa, O'Rourke decided to drive the short distance from Johannesburg to Soweto. By doing so, he knew that he was breaking South African law. It is illegal for a white person to enter Soweto without permission from the South African government.

Although he knew Soweto was just a few miles southwest of Johannesburg, O'Rourke was unable to find it. There were no exit signs marked "Soweto" on the expressway around Johannesburg. Determined not to give up, he left the highway and drove along a number of unpaved roads. Using the sun as a guide, he continued driving southwest, a direction that would surely lead him to the big city. Before long, he passed a tiny road sign that read SOWETO. He drove his car up a hill and suddenly saw before him rows and rows of drab little houses.

Here, at last, was the largest city in South Africa. Although the streets were crowded with people and the yards between the little homes were tiny, at first glance Soweto did not look like such a terrible place. Many of the homes had electricity and almost all had running water and modern sanitary facilities. In other countries, the reporter knew, some Africans seemed to live under worse conditions.

But beneath the surface, the problems of Soweto are enormous. The city was started in 1948 by the South African government. Whatever the official reasons for its creation, it was convenient to have a place close to Johannesburg where a large number of black Africans could live. Residents of the new city would do jobs few white people would consider taking. They could, for example, perform difficult and dangerous work in the white-owned gold mines around Johannesburg. They also could clean the homes of the wealthy white residents of the city.

As the years after 1948 passed, however, the white government of South Africa became concerned that so many black people lived so close to the comfortable neighborhoods of Johannesburg. The number of new homes built in Soweto was sharply restricted. As Soweto's population grew, more and more people had to squeeze into the tiny homes. By 1988, it was believed that each little house in Soweto had as many as thirty people living in it. The average age of the residents was close to twenty, a fact not recognized by the South African government.

In a sense, Soweto is a cross between a city and a huge prison. Until 1986, the residents of the city were not allowed to leave it for any reason without first obtaining written permission, a pass, from a white person, even a white child. In fact, a pass was needed by all South African black people to travel, to get a job, even to be outside at night. Over the years, literally millions of native Africans have been arrested simply because they did not have a proper pass. Nearly half of them were eighteen years old or younger. Since 1986, the laws have changed somewhat. But black South Africans know that travel in white neighborhoods without proper identification can still lead to arrest.

As he traveled through Soweto's crowded streets, reporter O'Rourke worried that some of the city's residents might resent the presence of a white stranger driving a shiny new car. For nearly an hour, with his car windows up and the doors locked, O'Rourke drove through the streets of Soweto. But to his surprise, he discovered that the people he drove by did not seem angry at all to see him. Many, in fact, were waving and smiling.

Back in the United States some months later, the reporter met an exchange student from Soweto. The student explained that the people of Soweto, seeing a white man driving alone there in a car, had assumed that he was an important civil rights leader. No other white person, they must have thought, would have had any reason to be there.

O'Rourke's visit to Soweto arose from professional curiosity. Like any good reporter, he wanted to learn everything he could about the subject he was studying, whether he was supposed to or not. But because he drove through the streets of Soweto without a guide, he knew nothing of the neighborhoods he passed through.

He may have known that Soweto was the home of one of the most famous families in South Africa. But he could not have known which of the little red brick houses nestled in the maze of streets was the home of Winnie Mandela, the wife of South Africa's imprisoned civil rights leader Nelson Mandela. Even if he had, he could not have visited Mandela.

At the time, Nelson Mandela had been away from his home and family for more than twenty-five years. With his seventieth birthday approaching, he had spent more than half of his adult life in South African prisons. He had been given a life sentence for sabotage and conspiracy to overthrow his country's government.

In any nation those would be serious charges. But despite them, or perhaps in part because of them, Nelson Mandela is the most honored prisoner in the world. He has been granted honorary doctoral degrees by universities from Africa to New York. Streets have been named in his honor in London, England, and in Grenoble, France. He has received the Jawaharlal Nehru Award from the Indian government, the Bruno Kreisky Prize for human rights, and Venezuela's Simón Bolívar Award. He has been formally honored by many cities and important societies.

But nowhere is he more revered today than in South Africa, his native land. There, for millions of black Africans and for many others as well, he is the symbol of resistance to the racial policies of the South African government. He is also the greatest source of hope for vast numbers of underprivileged people.

This is remarkable, because the South African government has done everything in its power to make Nelson Mandela as invisible and forgotten as his home city of Soweto. It has been illegal for years, for example, to publish anything

Mandela says or writes in a South African book, magazine, or newspaper. It is not even possible to see what he looks like. His last photograph was taken in 1965. During the first twenty-four years of his imprisonment, no one outside his prison was allowed to see him, with the exception of rare visits by his immediate family. During those infrequent gatherings, no one was permitted to discuss politics.

Nelson's wife Winnie has also felt the anger of the South African government. She was imprisoned for many months, alone in an otherwise empty jail cell. Later, she was forced to move from her home near Johannesburg to a faraway part of South Africa, living for years in what is called "internal exile." After the house she was forced to live in was bombed and burned, she returned to Soweto in defiance of government bans. For a time she was in grave danger of arrest and additional months or years of imprisonment. It is illegal for her to speak in public. These are just some of the ways the South African government has tried to silence the voices of first Nelson and later Winnie Mandela.

Those measures and many others were taken in a nation with a very delicate social structure. In South Africa, five million whites enjoy, by law, far more political, social, and economic power than twenty-eight million nonwhites.

These privileges, however, come with a price, even for the nation's ruling whites. For example, it is difficult for anyone, especially in South Africa, to learn about the lives and ideas of men like Nelson Mandela. Imprisoned for years and all but completely silenced, it has been rarely possible to ask Mandela questions about his youth and the decades he spent in jail. And yet the facts that are known, especially of his years as a young adult, paint a fascinating picture of a man and a movement.

During the late 1980s, South African laws about freedom of expression and news reporting have changed a great deal. If you happen to be in South Africa when you are reading this book, be sure to check current laws carefully. You could be in danger of arrest merely for having a book about Nelson Mandela. Even if you are not, you could be severely criticized by some South Africans who regard Nelson Mandela as little more than a common criminal. In the system they created, it is difficult to understand the true importance of Mandela's life and the movement he led.

Following twenty-seven-and-a-half years of imprisonment by the South African government, Nelson Mandela was released on Sunday, February 11, 1990. The event was covered in newspaper reports and television broadcasts around the world. In his first public speech in nearly three decades, Nelson said, "Our march to freedom is irreversible. We must not allow fear to stand in our way."

No longer "South Africa's *silent* voice of protest," Nelson Mandela met with President F.W. deKlerk in February 1990.

Chapter 2

PRINCE OF THE THEMBU

For centuries before Nelson Mandela was born, European colonists had fought with native Africans and each other to control the southern tip of the African continent. Within the boundaries of the modern nation of South Africa, a number of European colonies were established in the midst of native populations. European immigrants of Dutch ancestry, called Boers and later called Afrikaners, arrived first. They were followed by groups of English-speaking settlers. In 1814, the southernmost of the colonies, called Cape Colony, was purchased from the Dutch by Great Britain. As the number of English colonists increased and slavery was outlawed, many outraged Afrikaners moved northward to escape British rule.

Although both groups of Europeans had fought bloody battles with native Africans, the English-speaking residents of the Cape Colony seemed, at least for a time, to coexist with native Africans. For decades during the nineteenth century, black Africans and white European settlers alike took part in government and voted in general elections in the eastern part of the Cape Colony. For a few decades in the twentieth century, some blacks were allowed to vote as well, although increasingly strict property requirements gradually reduced their numbers.

In the Boer settlements to the north, however, the Europeans of Dutch ancestry were greatly distrustful of native Africans, with whom they had fought especially gruesome battles. There, from the very beginning, native Africans were given little opportunity to participate in government.

During the nineteenth century, the discovery of vast deposits of gold and diamonds in southern Africa complicated the colonial struggle. Europeans found it convenient to use native Africans for tough and dangerous work in the mines. Workers were obtained by a simple and cruel formula. Land was taken away from blacks by the better armed Europeans. Forced to live in areas inadequate for farming and cattle raising, the natives were nevertheless compelled to pay taxes. In order to pay the taxes, many native Africans were forced to work in the new mines and some of the other industries developing in southern Africa.

By the start of the twentieth century, the English-speaking colonists and the Dutch-speaking Boers were at war with each other. The South African war, sometimes called the Boer War, ended in 1902 with British forces victorious. For eight years, the various colonies of South Africa, including Boer and native African residents, lived under British rule. In 1910, the British Parliament declared the Union of South Africa an independent nation.

The new nation existed primarily for the benefit of white people. Black Africans, even those still allowed to vote in

Cape Province (formerly the Cape Colony), were regarded as laborers and third-class citizens. A black man passing a white person on the sidewalk, for example, was expected to tip his hat. If he did not, he was in danger of being attacked.

In reaction to this racist treatment, a number of black African leaders gathered in 1912 in the city of Bloemfontein to form the South African Native National Congress. The organization, later renamed the African National Congress (ANC), still exists today, but was banned for many years in South Africa. Mandela became its most famous leader.

Nelson Rolihlahla Mandela was born six years after the ANC was organized, on July 18, 1918, near a large village called Umtata. Umtata was, and remains, the capital of an African native reserve (or homeland) known as the Transkei. When the Union of South Africa was formed in 1910, the Transkei, which included an area known as Thembuland, was incorporated as part of the Cape Province, one of four South African provinces.

Nelson's first and last names, English in origin, show the influence of European settlers upon native African culture and language. But his middle name, Rolihlahla, is an African word meaning "stirring up trouble." Although the sophisticated culture the European settlers brought to South Africa had already greatly influenced South African natives, in at least some ways Nelson's youth was shaped by traditional African customs.

His father, Henry Gadla Mandela, was the second-most important leader of the Thembu tribe. He was also a close relative of the Thembu's paramount chief, David Dalindyebo. It was a custom among many native African leaders to have more than one wife. Henry had four, all of whom lived near one another in a group of whitewashed huts positioned around a cattle stockade called a *kraal*. Nelson's mother was a strong-willed woman named Nongaphi, usually called by a kind of nickname—Nosekeni.

One of the tragedies resulting from Nelson Mandela's decades of isolation is that little is understood about his earliest years. Nowhere has he described in any detail the village of his youth, nor has he been free to do so. It is known that the large Mandela family's kraal was located near the Mbashe River in the area of rolling hills and plains west of the Indian Ocean still known today as Thembuland. Following the traditional customs of the Thembu people, each of Henry Mandela's wives probably had several huts, one serving as a living room, another as a storeroom for grain and other supplies, yet another forming a kitchen. Like other Thembu family settlements, the Mandelas probably had a hut reserved for guests.

In many ways, the wealth of native African families was measured by the number of cattle each possessed. Cattle and sheep were allowed to graze in open pasturelands during the day. At night, they were herded into the family kraal. Children were often given the chore of gathering the cattle each evening, and Nelson Mandela undoubtedly helped his sisters with this task. As soon as he was old enough, he plowed fields and harvested crops as well.

As a member of the royal family of the Thembu, Henry Mandela often hosted meetings of the tribal elders. From a very early age, Nelson began listening to the discussions of the bearded, pipe-smoking old men, who often wore traditional robes and met in front of a huge log fire. When he was on trial in 1962, Nelson described those meetings:

"Many years ago, when I was a boy brought up in my village in the Transkei, I listened to the elders of the tribe telling stories about the good old days, before the arrival of the White man. Then our people lived peacefully, under the democratic rule of their kings and their 'amapakati' [advisers], and moved freely and confidently up and down the country without let or hindrance. Then the country was ours, in our own name and right. We occupied the land, the forests, the rivers; we extracted the mineral wealth beneath the soil and all the riches of this beautiful country. We set up and operated our own Government, we controlled our own armies and we organized our own trade and commerce. The elders would tell tales of the wars fought by our ancestors in defence of the fatherland, as well as the acts of valour performed by generals and soldiers during those epic days. . . .

"The structure and organization of early African societies

in this country fascinated me very much and greatly influenced the evolution of my political outlook. The land, then the means of production, belonged to the whole tribe, and there was no individual ownership whatsoever. There were no classes, no rich or poor and no exploitation of man by man. All men were free and equal and this was the foundation of government. Recognition of this general principle found expression in the constitution of the council, variously called Imbizo, or Pitso, or Kgotla, which governs the affairs of the tribe. The council was so completely democratic that all members of the tribe could participate in its deliberations. Chief and subject, warrior and medicine man, all took part and endeavoured to influence its decisions. It was so weighty and influential a body that no step of any importance could ever be taken by the tribe without reference to it."[1]

The democratic heritage of the Thembu people made living under any other type of government particularly difficult for many native Africans, including Nelson Mandela. But on the other hand, he clearly understood the limitations of the relatively simple culture of his people before the arrival of European settlers.

"There was much in such a society that was primitive and insecure," he said during the same 1962 trial, "and it certainly could never measure up to the demands of the present epoch. But in such a society are contained the seeds of revolutionary democracy in which none will be held in slavery or servitude, and in which poverty, want, and insecurity shall be no more."[2]

Although the South African government declared that the Transkei was a native reserve (in other words, for black people only), a number of white people lived there. Some were traders, who exchanged inexpensive manufactured goods for valuable minerals and animal goods obtained by the native Africans. Others were builders and land developers, who were already building resorts for whites along the Indian Ocean. Still others were missionaries, who established churches and schools for black Africans.

Nelson Mandela was among the Thembu children who began attending the missionary schools at an early age. He thus received two very different kinds of education. At home, he listened to the tales of the tribal elders, probably spoken in Xhosa, the native language of most South African blacks. He was expected to become a leader of the Thembu, and he was therefore often reminded of the important responsibilities that were ahead of him. The missionary schools, however, provided a very different type of learning.

At these schools, Nelson learned to read and write English, a subject he eventually mastered thoroughly. He read stories adapted from the Bible and from the history of southern Africa. The tales of early Christians made a lasting impact on his development. He became a devout Christian, as other members of his family had been for generations. His great-grandfather, Ngubengcuka, had once donated land to Christian missionaries so that they could build a high school. Nelson loved the Bible, but the same could not be said of the stories about African history that he read in school.

The history books used in the missionary schools were written by people of European heritage. The books referred to Thembu and other Xhosa-speaking warriors of the past as savages, barbarians, and cattle thieves. The fact that many Africans had died fighting bullets and artillery shells with just spears and wooden shields was hardly considered brave. Little mention was made of how the Europeans had written complex laws to take away cattle once owned and cared for by African blacks, and even the land they lived upon. The battles fought between natives and Europeans were called "Kaffir" wars. The word kaffir was used with contempt by white settlers describing native Africans.

Despite the often humiliating textbooks, Nelson Mandela realized from an early age that written languages were one of the great tools the Europeans used to advance their own civilizations. He hungered for knowledge about English, the language taught in the missionary school.

Although Nelson Mandela was an important Thembu leader, he and his family were poor. Nelson went to school wearing his father's hand-me-down clothes, far too large for his young body. Even though other children laughed at him, his sister, Mabel, recalled, Nelson hardly noticed their taunts. An English-language education was far more important to him.

For a time, the young man lived a relatively protected life. He performed chores around the family kraal. He listened to the Thembu elders discussing problems facing their people in preparation for his own leadership role. And he worked hard at the missionary school, learning English, mathematics, and the one-sided histories written by European settlers. But in 1930, when he was twelve years old, his life suddenly changed.

That year, his father became gravely sick. Understanding that death was near, the father gathered together his immediate family, including Nelson, and sent for David Dalindyebo, a close relative of the Mandelas and the paramount chief of the Thembu. When the highly respected chief arrived, Henry Mandela offered him his son. He hoped, no doubt, that Nelson's traditional Xhosa training could be continued as part of the royal family.

"I am giving you this servant, Rolihlahla," the dying man told the chief. "This is my only son. I can say from the way he speaks to his sisters and friends that his inclination is to help the nation. I want you to make him what you would like him to be; give him education, he will follow your example."[3]

The Thembu king agreed to his relative's request. Nelson

went to live at Mqekezweni, the Great Place of the Thembu chief.

Nelson Mandela spent the remainder of his adolescence as the adopted son of Chief David Dalindyebo. His body matured and he grew tall and athletic. He eventually grew to six feet four inches tall and was strong enough to enjoy some success as an amatuer boxer and long-distance runner. Since he lived with a king, it was hardly surprising that his natural self-assurance and air of authority grew stronger as well. Both traits, noted by almost everyone who knew him, stayed with him throughout his life, even through decades of imprisonment.

He continued his schooling at the Methodist Mission Center, a high school in Healdtown. There, he began to develop a mastery of English that eventually allowed him to speak clearly and eloquently in even the most emotionally charged situations. During the same period, he also listened to legal cases tried before his adopted father, Chief David Dalindyebo. Although the South African government took many steps to strip tribal leaders of their authority, the paramount chief of the Thembu still commanded the respect of his people. The cases brought to him by lesser chiefs, and tried carefully before him, awakened in Nelson an interest in the law that lasted a lifetime.

David Dalindyebo undoubtedly approved of his adopted son's activities. Although Nelson Mandela did not realize it at the time, the paramount chief was grooming him to one day assume his own role, king of the Thembu. In the language of Europeans, Nelson would be regarded as a crown prince. Had he known of the plans the chief had in mind for him, Nelson might well have been alarmed. He soon proved that he had no interest in becoming a king. He was more interested in a form of government called democracy.

Unfortunately, during the time he attended high school, a number of South African laws regarding native Africans were rewritten once again. They were altered so that the last remnants of true democracy were erased in Cape Province, where Nelson Mandela was born and raised. During a single year, the status of native Africans living under white rule in Cape Province changed from third-class citizens to much worse. The effects of the racist laws enacted in 1936, and others that soon followed, forever altered the course of the young man's life. At the time, he was eighteen years old.

In 1968, a black man shows his passbook in Johannesburg.

Chapter 3

THE YOUTH LEAGUE

In 1936, when Nelson Mandela was an eighteen-year-old student, the all-white legislature of South Africa voted overwhelmingly to pass a law called the Representation of Natives Act. The new law took away from those relatively few blacks living in Cape Province who still enjoyed it, the right to vote in the same elections as whites. Instead, native Africans were allowed to vote only in separate elections for a handful of white representatives to the national legislature. The possibility of black voters seriously changing national elections was completely minimized.

A second bill passed in 1936 was called the Native Trust and Land Act. At first glance, the new law seemed to help native Africans. It expanded the amount of land reserved for their use. But as with so many other South African laws, the so-called benefits to black people were deceiving. The bill actually formalized the white government's practice of simply taking away native land, a procedure that had been taking place for centuries. The law made it clear, for the first time, that Africa's black majority was expected to live on a tiny fraction of South Africa's total territory, less than thirteen percent of the land within the nation's borders.

During the same fateful year, the most hated of all South Africa's racist laws was brought to Cape Province for the first time. Until then, the infamous pass laws had been used throughout South Africa—with the exception of Cape Province. Now, all native African men living there, including Nelson Mandela, would need a written pass from a white person to travel anywhere, to be outside after dark, and to get a job.

Before 1936, native Africans living in Cape Province had not felt the full force of many laws written against them by European settlers. But as the harsh new restrictions took hold, especially the universally hated pass laws, resistance by native Africans in Cape Province increased dramatically. Among the many Africans who protested the increasingly unfair laws were students, including Nelson Mandela, who eventually found his student career thrown into chaos.

Probably in 1938, at the age of twenty, Nelson enrolled in the University College of Fort Hare. The school was located in the eastern part of Cape Province, in the village of Alice. At Fort Hare College, Nelson began studying for a bachelor of arts degree, his first formal step toward becoming a lawyer. At the school, he met a brilliant young African, Oliver Tambo, who was studying under an academic scholarship. The two students soon developed a friendship that lasted a lifetime. They also eventually formed the most famous native law firm in all of South Africa.

There is some confusion as to when Nelson actually began his college studies. His friend Oliver Tambo once wrote, "At the age of sixteen, Nelson went to Fort Hare and there we first met . . ."[1]

If he did attend the school at that early age, it would have been around 1934. However, several other writers indicate that Nelson began his studies at the college in 1938.

Regardless of when they began, Nelson's student days at Fort Hare College were cut short in 1940. As a member of the school's student council, he joined a strike protesting decisions by college authorities to lessen the organization's responsibilities. It was the first of many strikes Nelson would become involved in, and he quickly learned that such actions carried a heavy price. He and other strike leaders were promptly suspended from the college.

As soon as he left the college campus, Nelson returned to the Great Place of the paramount chief of the Thembu, his guardian. There, he found little sympathy from the Thembu chief, who ordered him to end his strike and return to his studies. At the same time, Nelson discovered that his guardian had major plans for him. He now learned, probably for the first time, that he was being trained to become paramount chief himself, and that a wife had been selected for him.

"My guardian felt it was time for me to get married," Nelson later said about the surprising development. "He loved me very much and looked after me as diligently as my father had. But he was no democrat and did not think it worth while to consult me about a wife. He selected a girl, fat and dignified; . . . and arrangements were made for the wedding."[2]

All at once, the young man was confronted with two commands he was reluctant to obey: to give up the student strike and to marry. He decided to solve both problems by leaving home and moving to the city of Johannesburg. At the time, he must have suspected that his new life would not be an easy one.

Traveling in a train car marked NON EUROPEANS, Nelson Mandela arrived in Johannesburg in 1941. At the time, many countries in Europe, Africa, and Asia were already involved in the early battles of World War II. Although many white Afrikaners openly supported the Nazi empire of Adolf Hitler, the South African government officially joined the side of the Allies united against Germany and Japan.

Because many South African men had entered the armed forces to fight in the war, jobs in Johannesburg were easy to find. Nelson quickly found a job as a private policeman with orders to guard the Crown Mines near Johannesburg. But he was forced to leave the mines when an agent for the Thembu chief found him and insisted he return to the Transkei.

Johannesburg, even in 1941, was a magnificent city, built upon the wealth of the world's richest gold mines and on the underpaid labor of native Africans. As a non-European, however, Nelson Mandela had little opportunity to enjoy life in the gleaming skyscrapers and comfortable suburbs of the city. Instead, he rented a room in the nearby township of Alexandria. Much like Soweto was about to become, only worse, Alexandria was a huge neighborhood of shacks and run-down homes inhabited by native Africans.

In Johannesburg and neighboring Alexandria, Nelson felt the pain of his first experiences living with native Africans in a major city. The black township was terribly over-crowded, and the residents were very poor. Worst of all were the constant raids by police, who actively searched for men whose pass papers were not in order.

Most of the residents of Alexandria earned a meager living by working for tiny wages at jobs in and around Johannesburg. Like his new neighbors, Nelson Mandela also needed a job in order to earn even a meager living. He soon met a man who, like himself and Oliver Tambo, was also from the Transkei native reserve, and who helped him greatly at a difficult time.

At the suggestion of a neighbor, Nelson visited Walter Sisulu, who operated a small real estate agency in Johannesburg. Sisulu had acquired his training through correspondence courses and now worked to find tiny patches of land that could still be sold legally to blacks.

Although Mandela introduced himself to Sisulu looking only for advice, the two young men seemed to respect each other from their first meeting. Sisulu offered Nelson a job in the real estate agency. Nelson accepted and soon explained his desire to become a lawyer. Sisulu encouraged him to continue his education by correspondence and gave him some financial help. Nelson soon acquired his BA degree.

Walter Sisulu proved to be a great friend. He gave Nelson enough money to buy a new suit for his graduation ceremony, and then introduced him to a group of white lawyers who operated a legal firm in Johannesburg. While he continued his studies at the University of Witwatersrand, Nelson worked at the legal firm as a kind of apprentice.

The young student soon found help from yet another source. While he was studying for his legal degree, he met and soon married a young nurse named Evelyn Ntoko Mase. Her work at the City Deep Mine Hospital provided enough income for her to help with Nelson's education. The newlyweds moved into a little house in another segregated township near Johannesburg. Orlando, as their new hometown was called, was renamed Soweto a few years later. Walter Sisulu and his wife Albertine lived in a nearby house.

From his home in Orlando, Nelson had to work, attend classes at the university, and return home before eleven in the evening. It was illegal for native Africans to be outside later than that hour. If he missed his train, or needed to work late at the library, he faced arrest merely for trying to get home.

Although these were the years of World War II, and South Africa was officially at war, many native Africans, including Nelson, were not drafted into the armed forces. The reason was simple. White South Africans were afraid to give guns to blacks. Many native Africans, who joined their country's army to fight against the racist government of Nazi Germany, faced terrible embarrassments when they discovered that they were not permitted to bear arms. It was injustices such as these, and many, many others, that eventually led Nelson Mandela to join the ANC.

Since its formation in 1912, just two years after the creation of the Union of South Africa, the ANC had served as the most persistent voice of organized native protest in the nation. But since 1936, when the racist policies of South Africa's white government were more firmly established on a national basis, many Africans felt growing dissatisfaction with the organization. After all, the ANC had existed for nearly a quarter of a century. Despite its efforts, conditions of native Africans had continually worsened.

Members of the ANC gave speeches and wrote articles explaining the many injustices of South Africa's racist policies. It was hoped that, by pointing out the wrongs of the white government and the suffering that the policies caused, South Africa's white politicians would change their ways. Unfortunately, the work of the ANC and other protest organizations had exactly the opposite effect. The European settlers seemed to become ever more afraid of African unrest and, in response, they passed laws that were more unfair and harsh.

In 1936, the very year that Africans in Cape Province were removed from voting roles and required to carry passes, the ANC reached a turning point. At its All-African Convention in Bloemfontein that year, some members suggested changing the organization's tactics. Instead of only talking about the need for liberation, some members began calling for direct action to make their demands for change more urgent. Many suggested a strike, in other words, a general refusal by blacks to work, for a time, in the white economy. However, a motion to change tactics was defeated at the 1936 convention. Since that time, interest in the ANC had been decreasing among Africans who felt its policies, however well intentioned, would not lead to change.

Throughout South Africa, black people felt the growing sting of the white government's racist policies. Probably no group felt it harder than men like Mandela, Walter Sisulu, and Oliver Tambo. They had grown up in relatively sheltered villages in the Transkei, only to move later to urban neighborhoods where racism reached its peak. Oliver Tambo had come to the Johannesburg area to teach school, and Nelson and his wife had moved to Orlando right next to the Sisulus. Two of Nelson's closest friends, therefore, were now living relatively close to him.

The three men met often to discuss the mutual problems they faced. To this group of three intelligent young men came a fourth, Anton Muziwakhe Lembede. Lembede was the son of poor Zulu farm workers who managed to become a teacher and then a lawyer. The four men, soon joined by Peter Mda and a number of others, discussed the possibility of making the African National Congress more vigorous. A way had to be found, each felt, to make the ANC's demands for change harder for the South African government to ignore. They finally agreed that some sort of mass movement, such as a nationwide work stoppage, was just the kind of action that would bring their demands to the attention of the government.

At the same time, Mandela and his friends realized that it would be difficult to change the basic policies of the ANC, which were almost exclusively educational. Rather than begin a policy battle with an organization they fundamentally respected, they decided to take a different tact entirely. They approached the ANC's president, Dr. A.B. Xuma, and proposed the creation of a Youth League as a separate organization within the ANC. Dr. Xuma accepted the proposal, although he was undoubtedly concerned about the wisdom of the actions the young men discussed.

During the first ANC Youth League elections held in April 1944, Anton Lembede was named president and Oliver Tambo secretary. Mandela, Mda, and a few others wrote a paper describing the policies of the new Youth League.

As outlined in the Youth League policy paper, the goals of the new organization were essentially democratic. The members called for the repeal of South Africa's racist laws. They demanded substantial changes in voting regulations so that native Africans could elect true representatives to the nation's legislature. The paper also called for land reform and free schools for children, as well as massive adult education programs.

The formation of the new Youth League and the development of its first policy paper, of course, had absolutely no effect on the white government. But for a time, many Africans felt renewed optimism that change would come. When the Nazi government of Hitler was completely destroyed in 1945, many Africans regarded it as a clear sign that racist policies were bound to fail throughout the world.

Tragically, at least in South Africa, just the opposite was true. In 1948, just three years after the end of World War II, a new political party came to power in South Africa. The National party, as it was called, was made up primarily of Dutch-speaking white Afrikaners, many of whom had supported the murderous racial policies of Adolf Hitler. The new party was quick to push through its own political agenda. The central theme of that policy was, and still is, called *apartheid*.

Many of the European settlers who advanced the apartheid theory felt that it was God's intention to keep the world's various races of people separate. Over the next few years, the National party created laws designed to do just that. The legal policy also ensured that native Africans would be forced to live in conditions decidedly inferior to whites.

The Prohibition Against Mixed Marriages Act soon was passed, providing harsh prison terms for people who married outside their own race. A complex system of regulations was developed in an attempt to clearly identify the race of every South African: black, colored (of mixed race), white, Indian, and so on, along with even finer distinctions. Under the law, each group was treated differently. The Population Registration Act was devised to make sure that every South African was given a strict racial definition by the government.

The Afrikaner Nationalist party created law after law to isolate and discriminate against nonwhite Africans. Under the Group Areas Act, a huge number of blacks were forced to move to often desolate and overcrowded areas approved for them by the government. The Urban Areas Act severely restricted the movements of blacks in cities, even breaking up families to ensure a sizable nonwhite work force was available near major cities. At the same time total black populations in urban areas were kept at a minimum. Even a new educational system was developed, in which blacks were to be taught subjects such as tree planting and singing instead of traditional school skills. Most resented by many native Africans was the new requirement to teach Afrikaans, a language of little worldwide significance, instead of English in the schools. Apartheid regulations soon became so complex that, were the results not so tragic, the whole affair would be laughable.

In a speech he wrote in 1953, Nelson Mandela described the effects of South Africa's racist laws on his native countrymen. He also referred to 1912, the year the African National Congress was formed:

"Since 1912 and year after year thereafter, in their homes, in provincial and national gatherings, on trains and buses, in the factories and on the farms, in cities, villages, shantytowns, schools and prisons, the African people have discussed the shameful misdeeds of those who rule the country.

"Year after year they have raised their voices to condemn the grinding poverty of the people, the low wages, the acute shortage of land, the inhuman exploitation, and the whole policy of White domination. But instead of more freedom, repression began to grow in volume and intensity and it seemed that all their sacrifices would end in smoke and dust."[3]

At about the same time apartheid was being formalized by the South African government, the African National

Congress and the ANC's Youth League began to lock horns on several important policy questions. A few years earlier, ANC leadership decided to join forces with the South African Indian Congress, an organization formed by Mahatma Gandhi in 1894, and the Communist party.

These new affiliations, especially with the Communist party, alarmed Nelson Mandela and others in the Youth League. Partly because of his upbringing as well as his Christian beliefs, Mandela was strictly opposed to communism. He also felt that Communists tended to view the problems of the world as a struggle between economic classes. It was clear to him that, at least in South Africa, the real problem was racism. With Tambo, Sisulu, and Lembede (until the latter's tragic death in 1947), he tried hard to make ANC members give up their ties with the Communist party. At the same time that they urged less talk with Communists, the Youth League members also urged campaigns of direct action to force changes in South African laws.

Mandela and his associates pointed out to older members of the ANC that mass demonstrations in South Africa were possible. Although the police retaliated brutally, native mine workers and South Africans of Indian heritage had organized huge demonstrations already. The ANC, they argued, could do the same, but on a far larger scale.

By the end of the 1940s, many members of the ANC were inclined to agree with the Youth League, which was becoming the leading voice of the entire congress. Soon, Peter Mda was elected league president, Oliver Tambo vice president, and Mandela, still a part-time law student, secretary. At around the same time, the leadership of the ANC was changed, as Dr. A.B. Xuma lost the presidential election to a younger man, Dr. James Moroka, who supported the Youth League's plans. Walter Sisulu was elected the ANC's secretary, and Mandela joined the congress's executive committee.

With new leadership, the official tactics of the African National Congress were quickly altered. Careful plans were made for the first direct action to be sponsored by the ANC, an action that leaders hoped would be joined by millions of native Africans. The congress called for a national work stoppage to be held on May Day, 1950. A turning point in the history of South African protest, filled with new hope and great danger, had been reached.

Chapter 4

THE STRUGGLE BEGINS

African National Congress leaders, now including Nelson Mandela and his friends, planned for a nationwide work stoppage to take place on May 1, 1950. But before the strike took place, members of South Africa's Communist party, as well as some other organizations, chose to support a strike in Johannesburg on the same day. The decision came as a shock to Mandela and other ANC leaders. They now found their first efforts at direct action protests aligned with a similar campaign organized by the Communist party.

Nelson Mandela was outraged that the carefully planned strike was suddenly adopted by Communists. He and a number of ANC associates stormed into Communist meetings around Johannesburg and created angry confrontations, forcing a number of them to break up in confusion. In a number of ANC Youth League publications, he criticized the Communist party in surprisingly harsh terms. But despite the unwelcome help of the Communists, Mandela and his co-workers continued making plans for the May Day strike.

When May 1 finally came, more than half of the native Africans in the Johannesburg area chose to join the strike and to stay home from work. But many of the striking workers gathered on the streets in front of their homes and work places. Unfortunately, several serious riots broke out as a result of the demonstration. The worst of the incidents was caused by police shootings. A number of native Africans were shot dead and dozens more were wounded. Realizing what was happening and concerned about trigger-happy police, Walter Sisulu and Mandela traveled through their township pleading with demonstrators to go home.

"That day was a turning-point in my life," Nelson said, "both in understanding through first-hand experience the ruthlessness of the police, and in being deeply impressed by the support African workers had given to the May Day call."[1]

A few months later, Mandela was elected president of the ANC Youth League, which by now was as widely known and respected as its parent organization. The new ANC Youth League president supported a second demonstration about two months later, but in many areas results were not as good as ANC members had hoped.

Primarily at the urging of Walter Sisulu, Mandela agreed to a major change in his position on ANC involvement in mass demonstrations. Previously, he had sought direct action almost exclusively by native Africans, who suffered most severely under South African law. But now he decided to appeal to all people and all races, including Indians, Asians, whites—and Communists. Although he did not agree with many of the political goals of communism, the increasingly severe laws of South Africa, coupled with harsh enforcement by police, compelled him to seek support from anyone willing to help.

In a sense, his decision played into the hands of the South African government. During the early 1950s, white politicians, police, and prosecutors began using a new law, called the Suppression of Communism Act, to arrest and harass leaders of African protest groups. The South African government, realizing that it had found an important new tool to use against black protest leaders, established a remarkably unusual definition of communism. According to South African law, a Communist was anyone who tried to bring about social or political change by creating a disturbance, by breaking a law, or by refusing to carry out certain duties.

Under this bizarre definition, a housewife who refused to buy bread from a local store that discriminated against Africans conceivably could be branded a Communist. By the same token, a mine worker who failed to report to work because of a disagreement with his boss, or more likely a planned ANC strike, also could be named a Communist.

As mad as it may have seemed, there was a clear purpose behind the government's wild definition of communism. White politicians in South Africa understood that many Europeans and Americans hated Communists and their ideals. By branding all native African protesters as Communists, the South African government felt that it could develop some support for its apartheid views in Europe and America. And many white South Africans felt the need for better relations with the rest of the world. In the United Nations as well as in individual foreign countries, South Africa's apartheid system was being criticized.

Soon after the Suppression of Communism Act was passed, the Communist party in South Africa disbanded, its former members moving their efforts underground. Now, it would be far more difficult for the South African government to keep tabs on them. White political leaders worried out loud that Communists and blacks might work together to murder whites, poison water supplies, and so on.

Some years later, while defending himself in court, Nelson Mandela explained the views of the ANC toward the Suppression of Communism Act:

"The ANC took the view that the Act was an invasion of the rights of our political organizations," he said, "that it was not only aimed against the Communist Party of South Africa, but was designed to attack and destroy all the political organizations that condemned the racialist policies of the South African Government. We felt that even if it were aimed against the Communist Party of South Africa we would still oppose it, because we believe that every political organization has a right to exist and to advocate its own point of view."[2]

By late 1951, many ANC leaders, including Nelson Mandela, decided to push harder for social change. In the past, one-day work stoppages had brought nationwide attention to ANC goals. But as always, government policies remained unchanged. Now, every conceivable form of protest, short of violence, was actively considered. Strikes and boycotts were, of course, possibilities, but Africans also could refuse to carry or show passes, stay outside after curfew, and attempt to enter areas reserved for "whites only," among other illegal but still peaceful actions.

In December 1951, the ANC held its yearly conference in Bloemfontein. It was decided that mass protest meetings against six selected apartheid laws would be scheduled for April 6, 1952. On that day, many white South Africans would be celebrating the three hundredth anniversary of the founding of the first Dutch settlement in southern Africa.

It was hoped that thousands of native Africans would use the day to listen to speeches by ANC activists, sing freedom songs, and join in prayers. In addition, the day might be used to find volunteers willing to prepare for more vigorous forms of protest. If at least some of the ANC's complaints about apartheid policies were not addressed by the government as a result of the meetings, further acts of civil disobedience were planned.

Collectively, the protests would be called the Defiance Campaign. Nelson Mandela was named the campaign's national volunteer-in-chief. It became his responsibility to choose volunteers to join the campaign and to see that each behaved peacefully and responsibly.

Walter Sisulu and ANC president Dr. Moroka wrote a detailed letter to the South African prime minister explaining the concerns of the ANC and asking the government to overturn a number of apartheid laws. The letter also announced the protest meetings scheduled for April 6 and warned that further actions of civil disobedience were planned, if necessary, to bring an end to the worst abuses of apartheid.

A blunt reply came from the prime minister's secretary. The secretary informed the ANC leaders that they should send all their letters not to the prime minister, but to the minister of native affairs. The letter went on to say that the government would not repeal apartheid law under any circumstances and made veiled threats about police actions against demonstrators.

While this correspondence was taking place, Nelson Mandela, often accompanied by Oliver Tambo, traveled by car to many black townships throughout a large portion of the country. He urged people, many of whom expressed concern about police reprisals, to attend the mass meetings scheduled for April 6. At all times he urged people to remain peaceful during the demonstration, to listen to prayers and speeches but to take no violent actions.

Huge crowds of native Africans, all entirely peaceful, gathered in a number of South African cities on April 6. The South African government gave no indication it planned to soften its apartheid laws, despite the huge numbers of Africans who attended mass meetings. Almost immediately, and exactly as promised, Nelson Mandela and other ANC leaders began signing up volunteers for the next stage in the defiance campaign, one that was far more dangerous than the first.

Each volunteer who agreed to join the campaign would be asked to defy a specific apartheid law. Many Africans were understandably reluctant to take part in an activity that could easily lead to arrest, beatings by police, harassment of family members, or even death. But Nelson continued to seek out those with the courage to take part in the dangerous acts of defiance.

During each meeting, sometimes with individual men and women, occasionally at gatherings of hundreds and even thousands of people, Mandela emphasized how every volunteer should behave during the campaign. He warned volunteers against showing even a hint of violence, bad temper, or drunkenness. He urged volunteers to wear clean, neat clothing, and to stand tall and erect regardless of the situations developing around them.

Joining native Africans in signing pledges to take part in the defiance campaign were South Africans of Indian heritage, who were also mistreated under South Africa's apartheid system. A handful of whites, ashamed of the system other European settlers had established, also decided to join the demonstration.

The campaign of defiance began on June 26, 1952, the second anniversary of the ANC's national strike. In his famous speech entitled *No Easy Walk to Freedom*, Mandela described the results of the campaign:

"Factory and office-workers, doctors, lawyers, teachers, students, and the clergy; Africans, Coloureds, Indians, and Europeans, old and young, all rallied to the national call and defied the pass laws and the curfew and the railway apartheid regulations. By the end of the year, 8,500 people of all races had defied. The Campaign called for immediate and heavy sacrifices. Workers lost their jobs, chiefs and teachers were expelled from the service, doctors, lawyers, and businessmen gave up their practices and businesses and elected to go to jail. Defiance was a step of great political significance. It released stronger social forces which affected thousands of our countrymen."[3]

Mandela himself was arrested on June 26, during the very first evening of the campaign, while addressing a meeting in Johannesburg. When the eleven P.M. curfew for blacks arrived and the meeting continued, he and other volunteers were promptly arrested and moved into waiting police vans.

Jailed for the first time in his life, Mandela was given an

eyewitness view of police brutality. A fellow volunteer was pushed by a policeman down a flight of stairs. Despite the fact that the African had obviously broken his ankle, he was refused medical attention at police headquarters. Mandela was eventually released from police custody, but his legal problems with the South African government were just beginning.

"I would say that the whole life of any thinking African in this country drives him continuously to a conflict between his conscience on the one hand and the law on the other . . ." Mandela stated while on trial in 1962. "The law as it is applied, the law as it has been developed over a long period of history, and especially the law as it is written and designed by the Nationalist Government, is a law which, in our view, *is immoral, unjust, and intolerable.* Our consciences dictate that we must protest against it, that we must oppose it, and that we must attempt to alter it."[4]

Like other members of the ANC, Mandela was now entering a period when his conscience and South African law would collide almost continuously. For the rest of his life, arrest and imprisonment stood as significant threats and, all too soon, harsh realities.

Little more than a month after the start of the defiance campaign, Mandela and many of his associates found their homes and offices raided by police. Along with Walter Sisulu and more than thirty other ANC leaders and volunteers, Mandela was arrested once again, this time under the terms of the Suppression of Communism Act. Although he was released from police custody, he now faced a court date near the end of November to answer the charges of promoting Communist goals.

In the meantime, the defiance campaign moved into its final and largest phase. The ANC urged Africans by the millions to disobey selected apartheid regulations. Thousands of people were arrested for defying South African law. Dozens of unarmed protesters were killed by police bullets.

In response to what it considered a growing threat from Africans, Indians, and a handful of whites, the government began a severe crackdown. Police, the army, and other authorities were given powers of martial law, in which the few civil rights of South Africans were suspended. People who broke apartheid laws faced whippings and long prison terms. Passive resistance in any form, as a kind of protest, was declared illegal. The defiance campaign was finally stopped when the government banned more than fifty of the movement's leaders.

Over the next few years, most South African protest organizers would feel the effects of government bans. At first, when a person was banned, he or she was confined to a particular area of the country, usually a city or village, sometimes far from home. Even more significantly, banned persons were forbidden to talk with more than one or two people at a time, making it impossible for them to attend any types of meetings. Banning orders could be issued without a trial, and violators faced years of imprisonment. Gradually, banning orders became longer and more complex, with even more aspects of personal behavior restricted by the government.

Mandela, Sisulu, and other ANC defiance campaign leaders were brought to trial late in November 1952. To the disappointment of government prosecutors, the trial judge pointed out that the ANC leaders were not guilty of true communism, only of "statutory communism" as defined so broadly by South African law. Noting that the campaign organizers had always asked their followers to remain peaceful, the judge handed down suspended sentences. He also warned Mandela and the others not to repeat their offenses. With this warning, the leaders were allowed to leave.

For the time being, at least, Mandela and his ANC associates were free to consider new forms of protest. Much work was needed. The government crackdown had brought the defiance campaign to a grinding halt. Despite all the work, not a single apartheid law had been taken off the books.

Mandela and his supporters singing during the first treason trial in 1956

Mandela talks with Ruth First outside the courthouse. Ruth First, also a member of the ANC, was killed by a letter bomb in 1982.

Above: A concerned woman talks to Winnie Mandela outside the court after Nelson was sentenced to life imprisonment. Below left: Robben Island, the maximum security prison, is seven miles off the coast of Cape Town. It is claimed that the water is very icy and no one has survived the swim to freedom. Below right: In 1960, dead and wounded lie in the street after the police fired on a stone-throwing crowd protesting the need to carry identification passes.

A 1971 photo shows an overcrowded nursery facility in Soweto.

Above: Policemen amid the bodies of victims of the Sharpeville massacre
Right: Tear gas disperses a crowd of jeering students in 1977.

Above: Gold miners eating their dinner in their living quarters.
Below: Militant miners at a memorial service for 177 employees who died in an underground fire (left). A striking miner injured by security guards' rubber bullets (right)

Above left: Albert Lutuli, winner of the Nobel Peace Prize in 1960
Above right: Supporters of jailed leader Mandela at a mass meeting
near Port Elizabeth in 1986. Below: Dr. Oliver Tambo (right), president
of the ANC, receives the Third World prize from the prime minister of
Malaysia on behalf of Winnie and Nelson Mandela.

Left: Winnie Mandela, in 1988, urges university students to unite in the struggle against apartheid.

Below: Winnie, and her daughters, Zeni (left) and Zindzi (right)

Above: Winnie Mandela leaving her home in Brandfort after it was damaged in an arson attack. With her are her daughter, Zindzi, and the family lawyer, Ismail Ayob.

Right: In 1985, Zindzi reads her father's refusal to leave prison after President P.W. Botha offered him conditional release.

Above: Celebrating Mandela's seventieth birthday, students wave posters and sing freedom songs. Below: A Soweto township police officer drags away a woman after a demonstration in 1987.

In 1952, a group who defied apartheid laws are arrested. In the truck, on the extreme right, is Walter Sisulu.

Chapter 5

THE GOVERNMENT CRACKDOWN

It is a testament to Nelson Mandela's determination and hard work that, in addition to his job and to his work in the African National Congress, he was able to finish his formal education and become a full-fledged lawyer. He had studied at Witwatersrand University and the University of South Africa, and, although he studied under black teachers, had passed the same bar exams that white students took.

In 1952, the same year he organized volunteers for the defiance campaign, he opened up a legal office with his friend and ANC associate Oliver Tambo. The office was in a run-down building called Chancellor House near the Johannesburg court building.

"Chancellor House in Fox Street was one of the few buildings in which African tenants could hire offices," Tambo wrote in 1964, "it was owned by Indians. This was before the axe of the Group Areas Act fell to declare the area 'White' and landlords were themselves prosecuted if they did not evict the Africans. MANDELA AND TAMBO was written huge across the frosted window panes on the second floor, and the letters stood out like a challenge. To White South Africa it was bad enough that two men with black skins should practise as lawyers, but it was indescribably worse that the letters also spelled out our political partnership."[1]

Oliver Tambo went on to describe the day-to-day workings of the law offices he shared for years with Nelson. He explained that, each morning, both lawyers found crowds of people already gathered in the waiting room and overflowing into the hallways seeking legal help. Some clients had committed serious crimes. Tambo noted that violent offenses were on the rise in South Africa's apartheid society. But he also noted that many defendants needed protection from minor charges and unjust laws.

Nelson Mandela was now forced to pursue most of his protest efforts in courtrooms ruled by white judges. Like many other ANC leaders, he had been banned for his activities during the defiance campaign. He was restricted to the Johannesburg area, forbidden to attend meetings, and, a few months later, ordered to resign from the African National Congress, in which he had risen to the position of president of the large Transvaal Province chapter.

With few breaks, he was issued increasingly restrictive banning orders until he was imprisoned for life. While still a free man, although regularly followed by policemen, he risked arrest often by speaking to ANC gatherings. But in 1953, when he was scheduled to deliver an address at the annual ANC meeting, his famous speech *No Easy Walk to Freedom* had to be read by an associate in his name.

Although he and most other ANC leaders were banned from attending meetings, Mandela nevertheless developed a tactic, called the M plan, for organizing ANC activities. "Mandela drafted the M plan," Oliver Tambo remembered more than a decade later, "a simple commonsense plan for organization on a street basis so that Congress volunteers would be in daily touch with the people, alert to their needs and able to mobilize them."[2]

Nelson's scheme called for ANC volunteers to meet secretly with other people, in homes, trains, work places, or any location where police suspicions would not be aroused. Although it smacked of conspiracy, the plan was necessitated by the policies of the South African government. Mandela and other ANC leaders would certainly have preferred to attend free and open gatherings, as they had in the past, to consider more forms of nonviolent protest. But government banning orders prohibited them and most other ANC leaders.

While all of this was going on, Nelson continued working at his busy legal practice. When he was defending himself in court years later, Mandela described his experiences as a lawyer in partnership with Oliver Tambo. "In the courts where we practised we were treated courteously by many officials," he said, "but we were very often discriminated against by some and treated with resentment and hostility by others. We were constantly aware that no matter how well, how correctly, how adequately we pursued our career of law, we could not become a prosecutor, or a magistrate, or a judge. We became aware of the fact that as attorneys we often dealt with officials whose competence and attainments were no higher than ours, but whose superior position was maintained and protected by a White skin.

"I regarded it as a duty which I owed, not just to my people, but also to my profession, to the practice of law, and to justice for all mankind, to cry out against this discrimination which is essentially unjust . . . I believed that in taking up a stand against this injustice I was upholding the dignity of what should be an honourable profession."[3]

In 1954, the local law society tried to disbar Mandela for his activities during the defiance campaign, but the attempt was unsuccessful. Far more successful were the efforts of government authorities and police to disrupt his efforts aimed at organizing African protests. Although he illegally attended a few meetings, Mandela threw much of his energy into writing articles outlining the abuses of apartheid. Between June 1953 and May 1959, many of his essays appeared in *Liberation*, a monthly journal sponsored by the ANC.

In some of the articles he wrote for *Liberation*, Mandela noted the increasingly horrible effects of apartheid law. In addition to many other abuses, he pointed out, the cruel laws were being used to break up African families.

Under the Group Areas Act, whole African villages were destroyed by bulldozers, the inhabitants forced to move to areas reserved by the government for natives. But land on the reserves was often poor and severely limited, insufficient for residents to use as farmland and cattle ranges. So the people faced what their ancestors faced in the 1800s. It was impossible for even a sizable minority of resettled Africans to fall back on their traditional farm economy. To earn a living, and to pay taxes imposed by the government, it was necessary for many African men to work in white-owned factories and, especially, South Africa's huge gold and diamond mines.

Tragically, the Group Areas Act did not permit many black families to live close enough to mines and other job sites to allow daily commutes by workers. For the majority of each year, therefore, many African laborers were forced to leave behind their wives and children and to move into crowded, military-style barracks near the mines. Payment blacks received for their hard and dangerous work was far less than that given even unskilled whites for easier labor. The money workers sent home was insufficient to keep their families from suffering the effects of malnutrition and disease. The vicious policy made some black men turn to crime.

In a 1956 edition of *Liberation*, Mandela discussed a number of apartheid restrictions and wrote that "the real purpose of the scheme is to increase land hunger for the masses of the peasants in the reserves and to impoverish them. The main object is to create a huge army of migrant labourers ... By enclosing them in compounds at the centres of work and housing them in rural locations when they return home, it is hoped to prevent the emergence of a closely knit, powerful, militant and articulate African industrial proletariat who might acquire the rudiments of political agitation and struggle. What is wanted by the ruling circles is a docile, spineless, unorganized and inarticulate army of workers."[4]

With most of its leaders banned and its members more impoverished than ever, the African National Congress continued to struggle as best it could against the white South African government. In the village of Kliptown southwest of Johannesburg, several thousand delegates attended a meeting, called the Congress of the People, on June 25, 1955. The most important outcome of the two-day affair was a document, called the Freedom Charter, that outlined the rights of all South Africans, regardless of race.

Although they were banned from attending meetings such as the Congress of the People, both Mandela and Walter Sisulu approved the final wording of the Freedom Charter. Briefly, the document called for equal political, economic, and social rights for all South Africans, equal protection for all people under the law, land and educational reform, and peace and friendship between the races.

During the Congress of the People, the Freedom Charter was read in English as well as in native African languages.

The large crowd attending the meeting roared its approval as each section was read. But on the second day, a huge force of armed police arrived, taking away every written document that could be found. As the raid was taking place, the large crowd began to sing a patriotic song.

The demands of Nelson's legal profession and his behind-the-scenes protest work, coupled with almost constant harassment by police, soon caused problems in his personal life. Since his student days, Nelson had been married to Evelyn Ntoko Mase (who became Evelyn Mandela). During the years of her marriage to Nelson, Evelyn gave birth to two boys, Thembekile and Makgatho, and a daughter, Makaziwe. But the increasingly difficult struggle in which her husband was involved made life exceptionally difficult for her.

For a time, she and the children were away from their Orlando home while Evelyn pursued additional nursing training. Eventually, Evelyn decided to take the children and move away from Nelson, Orlando, and the daily controversies that made a normal life difficult at best. The couple eventually divorced.

The breakup of his family was not the only problem faced by Nelson Mandela, or other native Africans either. The South African government continued to pass more severe apartheid laws. Among other actions, it extended the pass laws to females in 1956. Despite protests by thousands of African women, the new pass laws remained in effect.

Worse yet, government officials refused to forget the simple demands for fair treatment for all residents of South Africans made in the Freedom Charter. Police raided the homes and offices of thousands of people suspected of having anything to do with the ANC, the Congress of the People, or the protest movement in general.

The raids reached a peak during the night of December 4-5, 1956, when 137 men and 19 women, including blacks, coloreds, Indians, and nearly two dozen whites, were arrested and charged with treason. The police took into custody people at the highest levels of the ANC leadership, including Chief Albert Lutuli, the Congress's current president and a man who, a few years later, would win the Nobel Peace Prize.

Nelson Mandela was awakened and arrested at his home near dawn on the morning of December 5. Like the other people arrested at nearly the same time, he was charged as a Communist conspirator attempting to overthrow the government by violent means. Every defendant, if convicted, faced the possibility of the death penalty.

Through the use of elaborate banning orders, the South African government had gone to considerable trouble to prevent leaders of the ANC from meeting. Now it brought them all together in two large prison cells, one for Europeans, the other for non-Europeans, in an ancient Johannesburg prison. Mandela, Lutuli, Tambo, Sisulu, and 152 others at last could communicate with each other, although under wretched and overcrowded conditions.

Two weeks later, all the defendants, loudly singing freedom songs, were herded into a packed Johannesburg courtroom. From the outset, the government demonstrated total incompetence. A broken microphone made it impossible to begin proceedings on the first day. On the second day, court officials decided to force all the defendants into a huge steel cage. Defense attorneys refused to continue until the cage was removed. While that was being done, government incompetence resulted in tragedy.

Despite the fact that 156 people were on trial for their lives, the atmosphere among the defendants inside the courtroom, as well as among spectators gathered outside the building, was gay and festive. Many of the spectators danced and sang African songs, which were misunderstood by a number of white policemen standing guard outside the building. To the horror of the police colonel in charge, a number of his men opened fire on the peaceful crowd. More than twenty people were injured.

When it began, few people suspected that the Treason Trial, as it became known, would drag on for about four and a half years. But it did. Although some of the defendants were released after the first twelve months, Nelson was among those kept on trial for the duration. State prosecutors were determined to find a violent Communist conspiracy where in fact none existed. Looking for evidence, they studied every printed document written or possessed by every defendant from 1952 to 1956.

Although the government at one point considered the defendants dangerous enough to lock in a courtroom cage, cooler heads soon prevailed. Nelson and the other defendants were granted bail, enabling them to leave the courtroom every evening and to enjoy some semblance of freedom when court was not in session.

Everyone on trial, especially those far away from home, found their lives completely disrupted for as long as four years. Mandela and Tambo were fortunate because they lived and worked close enough to the courthouse to continue their practice during the evenings and when court was not in session. For two famous defenders of civil liberties in an apartheid society, business was better than brisk.

Strangely enough, the years of the Treason Trial seem to be among the happiest of Nelson Mandela's life. Forbidden to speak at meetings, he soon found an increasingly wide audience for his views, which he was soon commanded to deliver at length in the Johannesburg courtroom. It was during this trial too that he met and married Winnie Madikizela, beginning one of the most famous, and tragic, romances of our times.

Chapter 6

NOMZAMO WINNIE

The woman who eventually became Nelson Mandela's second wife, and an important political leader in her own right, was born in 1936 in a mountainous region of the Transkei known as Pondoland. Her full Xhosa name was Nkosikazi Nobandle Nomzamo Madikizela, but her parents, both teachers, gave her the additional European name Winifred. She is known throughout the world today as Winnie.

At school, she was a superb student, always at the top of her class. Fortunately, she was educated in classical subjects such as Latin, mathematics, and science just before apartheid laws were changed to require black students to learn skills like tree planting and singing. Outside of school, Winnie was somewhat of a tomboy, athletic, proud, and self-assertive. She also grew to be quite beautiful. Before long, a number of suitors, including Nelson Mandela, would regard her as anything but a tomboy.

Winnie Madikizela first heard of Nelson Mandela's activities during the defiance campaign while she was still in high school. Like so many other informed native Africans, she continued to follow his struggle, although at the time he knew nothing of her. She moved to Johannesburg in 1953, where she studied social work at the Jan Hofmeyr Social Center. One of the prominent patrons of the Hofmeyr school, his name listed on all school letterheads, was Nelson Mandela.

For a time, Winnie felt ill at ease among the city people in Johannesburg. Although she considered herself a "country bumpkin," she managed to earn top marks at the Hofmeyr school. After she was graduated in 1955, she became South Africa's first black medical social worker, thus becoming somewhat of a celebrity herself. Late in the year, she began working and continuing her training in Johannesburg's Baragwanath Hospital for Africans. She pursued her work with diligence, searching through black townships on her own time, looking for people in particular need of help. She lived at a hostel.

Nelson was not aware of his future wife's first glimpse of him. "I saw Nelson Mandela for the first time in the Johannesburg Regional Court," Winnie remembered years later. "He was representing a colleague of mine who had been assaulted by police. I just saw this towering, imposing man, actually quite awesome. As he walked into court, the crowd whispered his name."[1]

She finally met Nelson through her friend Adelaide Tsukudu, who was dating, and soon married, Nelson's legal partner Oliver Tambo. Adelaide, like Winnie, lived at the Helping Hand Club hostel. Winnie and Oliver were from the same Transkei village, called Bizana, but they just barely knew one another.

During a recess in the Treason Trial, Oliver and Adelaide were driving down the street in Oliver's old blue car. They spotted Winnie, who had just left Baragwanath Hospital, on the sidewalk near a bus stop reading a book. Adelaide offered Winnie a lift back to the hostel, saying that they were first going to stop for some food. When they arrived at the takeout restaurant, they spotted Nelson standing at the counter.

Adelaide walked into the store. "Buy whatever you want and be sure to get Nelson to pay," Oliver joked. When Adelaide and Nelson walked out together, Oliver introduced his partner to Winnie. He also referred to the fact that photos of Winnie had often been featured in African publications. "Winnie is also from Bizana," he told Nelson, "surely you have seen her pictures in *Bantu World* and *Drum*—she is always dancing about their pages."[2]

Winnie felt shy and awkward around two such famous political leaders. She thought that Nelson had barely noticed her. But he had, and he called her the next day at her hospital office.

"He invited me to lunch and said he would send a friend to fetch me," Winnie recalled. "I was of course petrified—he was much older than me and he was a patron of my school of social work. We had never seen him, he was just a name on the letterheads; he was too important for us students to even know him. So when I got this call, I couldn't work for the rest of the day. And when I prepared to go and meet him, I took out every schoolgirl's dress I possessed. Nothing seemed suitable—in those days we had almost knee-length frilled dresses that made one look even younger and more ridiculous. And when I ultimately found something more dignified—it wasn't even mine. I felt so uncomfortable.

"It was a Sunday. He always worked right through—Saturdays, Sundays, Mondays, the days were the same. I was driven to his office where he was buried in files, there were stacks and stacks of files all over, and it was just about lunch-time."[3]

When they arrived at the restaurant, they ordered spicy Indian dishes, Winnie's first taste of such hot food. A quiet talk was impossible. Throughout the meal, people approached Nelson asking for advice and legal help. Even without the interruptions, Winnie would not have been able to manage a normal conversation. Her mouth was on fire from the Indian spices! She wondered how Nelson could enjoy such food. It took a half hour to walk from the restaurant to Nelson's nearby car, because he insisted on answering questions from everyone who approached him.

Despite his busy schedule, Nelson found the time to visit Winnie often. He also sent friends to bring her to him at any moments he could take away from his legal work or his time planning the Treason Trial defense. She was even brought to a gymnasium to sit and watch him work out.

76

Finally, on March 10, 1957, while they were driving in his car, Nelson asked her to marry him. As Winnie remembered, he worded the request somewhat peculiarly.

"One day, Nelson just pulled up on the side of the road and said, 'You know, there is a woman, a dressmaker, you must go and see her, she is going to make your wedding-gown. How many bridesmaids would you like to have?' That's how I was told I was getting married to him! It was not put arrogantly; it was just something taken for granted. I asked, 'What time?'"[4]

Nelson Mandela managed to obtain a four-day pass from his banning orders so that he and Winnie could travel to Pondoland to be married in the village of the brides' parents. They were married at the Methodist church in Bizana on June 14, 1958. Because of arrangements made by Winnie's father, the huge reception was held in Bizana's town hall, the first time the building had ever been used by native Africans.

Although custom dictated that the couple travel on to Nelson's childhood home, the groom's four-day pass did not allow it. Winnie has saved a piece of the wedding cake for thirty years in the hope that the custom can one day be completed.

Most native African residents of Soweto, and other localities, cannot own their own homes. They must rent them from the government. Nelson was granted the right to rent for life his home in a Soweto township called Orlando West. By neighborhood standards, it was a better than average house. It had electricity, running water, a telephone, and an inside bathroom.

Houses in South African black townships do not have real street addresses, just numbers. Mandela's house was No. 8115. Nelson and Winnie moved into No. 8115 right after their marriage.

Unfortunately, that number was already well known by local police. On one of their first nights together, the newlyweds were awakened by the pounding of clubs on their door. It was Winnie's first experience of a police raid.

"There were these coarse Boer policemen thumbing through our personal belongings, pulling books off shelves, turning drawers of clothing upside down, reading our letters, rough handling our possessions and all the time passing derogatory and derisory remarks about kaffirs. It was horrible. And it was all for nothing. They couldn't find anything incriminating. After they had gone we tidied up the mess and I made coffee before we went back to bed. Nelson warned me I would have to get used to raids like that . . ."[5]

The Treason Trial resumed on August 1, 1958. This time, the proceedings were moved to South Africa's capital, Pretoria, about forty miles from Johannesburg. Almost immediately, the charges against sixty-one defendants, including Chief Lutuli and Oliver Tambo, were dropped. Charges against Mandela, Walter Sisulu, and eighty-nine others stayed in force. Mandela and some of the other defendants drove together to the trial each day, keeping their spirits high by telling jokes and stopping at roadside fruit stands.

Winnie, who in describing her marriage to Nelson had frequently noted that "life with him was always life without him," found herself without her husband much of each day. She joined the ANC Women's League and the Federation of South African Women, and soon paid the price for her political activities.

In October 1958, she joined a march to protest the apartheid pass laws. She was imprisoned, pregnant, in a filthy Johannesburg jail for a month. When she was released, she was told that she had been fired by Baragwanath Hospital for her activities. Fortunately, friends helped her find another job as a social worker at the well-known Johannesburg Child Welfare Society, where she worked with brief maternity leaves for four years. Her first child, a daughter named Zenani, was born in 1959.

Early that same year, on January 19, the South African government once again demonstrated its incompetence in the Treason Trial. Unable to produce evidence against 61 additional defendants, it was forced to drop the charges against them. Of the original 156 accused of a Communist conspiracy, only 30, including Mandela and Walter Sisulu, remained on trial.

During the following year, 1960, government agents also demonstrated their murderous cruelty. The Pan-African Congress, a political group that had split away from the ANC in a policy disagreement, called for massive demonstrations against the pass laws. At Sharpeville, a black township south of Johannesburg, a number of Pan-African Congress volunteers gathered in front of a police station without carrying their passes. Local residents, curious about the demonstration, joined the crowd.

Watching the protesters perform traditional songs and dances, newspaper reporters present indicated that the gathering was peaceful, even happy. But police inside the station disagreed. A squad of seventy-five armed policemen lined up outside the building and opened fire on the unarmed crowd. At least seven hundred shots were fired, most as the demonstrators were already running away. Sixty-nine protesters were killed, nearly two hundred wounded. Most were shot in the back. In a similar incident at the town of Langa, forty-nine people were wounded and two were killed.

The African National Congress called for a strike as part of a day of mourning. Chief Lutuli, in a public demonstration, burned his passbook. Thousands of other Africans followed his lead. For a moment, stung by a barrage of worldwide criticism, the South African government wavered. Briefly, it suspended the pass laws. But then, as it had so many times in the past, the government cracked down hard.

A state of national emergency was declared. The African National Congress and the Pan-African Congress were banned. The organizations were banned for thirty years.

Throughout the country, police began one of the most massive roundups in South African history. About eighteen hundred political leaders were put in prison. As part of the crackdown, bail for defendants in the Treason Trial was revoked. Mandela and the others now went from the courtroom to an overcrowded and dirty Pretoria jail cell each day. They were offered food unfit to eat. They remained imprisoned throughout the spring and summer of 1960.

The well-known team of defense lawyers angrily quit the trial, declaring that it was impossible to defend their clients under conditions of hysteria. The Pretoria prisoners elected Mandela as their spokesman. With Walter Sisulu and a few others, he prepared their continuing defense.

Winnie attended the trial whenever possible. She heard her husband speak eloquently for days, often answering pointed questions put to him by white court officials.

When asked by a judge if his freedom was a threat to Europeans, Nelson replied: "No, it is not a direct threat to the Europeans. We are not anti-White, we are against White supremacy . . . before we launched the Defiance Campaign, we said that the campaign we were about to launch was not directed against any racial group. It was a campaign which was directed against laws which we considered unjust, and

81

time without number the ANC has explained this . . . It is quite clear that the Congress has consistently preached a policy of race harmony and we have condemned racialism no matter by whom it is professed."[6]

The nationwide South African State of Emergency was finally lifted at the end of August. The Treason Trial prisoners at last could post bail and return home when court was not in session. During the Christmas holidays, Nelson visited his family. When he learned that Makgatho, his son from his first marriage with Evelyn, had become sick, he risked arrest by rushing to the Transkei to be with him. Soon, he had to rush back to Johannesburg, after learning that Winnie had given birth to a second daughter, Zindziswa.

The Treason Trial dragged on into 1961, more than four years after it had started. One by one, leaders of the African protest movement calmly answered questions. Just as Mandela had testified, they confirmed the fact that the demonstrations organized by the African National Congress were neither violent nor inspired by Communist goals. State prosecutors, having read thousands of printed ANC documents, could find no substantial evidence to the contrary.

On March 29, 1961, the day set aside for the verdict finally arrived. The remaining defendants, including Mandela and Walter Sisulu, waited quietly. The room was packed with spectators and reporters.

Justice Rumpff, the senior judge in the long case, began

by making a series of remarks. He said that the ANC was trying to form a new kind of government in South Africa. He also noted that the Program of Defiance had urged people to break the law. However, he felt that prosecutors had not shown that the ANC encouraged violence. And although the Congress accepted both Communist and non-Communists as members and leaders, the state had not shown that its goals were inspired by communism.

Judge Rumpff ordered the defendants to stand. Then he addressed them by saying, "You are found not guilty and discharged. You may go."

After four and a half years of struggle, Mandela, Sisulu, and the other defendants were free—to an extent. Because of his banning orders, in effect nearly uninterrupted for nine years, Nelson could not legally leave the Johannesburg area. Nor could he address meetings. The African National Congress, the focus of his political efforts for many years, had been banned.

Still, the verdict was a victory of the defendants, who sang a freedom song outside the Pretoria court building. Of the 156 people accused in the early days of the Treason Trial, not a single one was convicted.

With the trial over at long last, Winnie Mandela may have thought briefly that she would see more of her husband for a time. But immediately she discovered the truth of her own statement: "Life with him was always life without him."

Nelson Mandela after his acquittal in the long Treason Trial

Chapter 7

UMKHONTO WE SIZWE

The story of events surrounding Nelson and Winnie Mandela at the end of the long Treason Trial is somewhat confused. In the excitement, Winnie herself may have forgotten some of the details. There are a number of conflicting accounts, all of which seem to be based, at least in part, on information she provided.

Winnie was in the Pretoria courtroom when the not-guilty verdict was given. She then returned to the Orlando West house and was soon met by either Walter Sisulu or, more probably, Nelson himself—on this point there are two different accounts. She was told to pack a few things in a suitcase for Nelson, and may or may not have been told that he had to leave for a long time. In still a third account, Nelson decided to leave his home and legal practice before the final verdict was given, returning to the court each day from an underground hiding place until the conclusion of the trial.

At any rate, it is clear that the banned leader of the banned ANC had decided to change his tactics. As evidenced by the earlier M plan, and now by his decision to exist in hiding away from police surveillance, Nelson clearly had determined that life within the law was impossible for him. He had decided, probably in consultation with other banned ANC leaders, to live the life of an outlaw. He must have reached the decision with great sorrow. In yet another trial a year later, he described his feelings at moving underground.

"It has not been easy for me during the past period to separate myself from my wife and children . . . and instead to take up the life of a man hunted continuously by the police . . . This has been a life infinitely more difficult than serving a prison sentence. No man in his right senses would voluntarily choose such a life in preference to the one of normal, family, social life which exists in every civilized community.

"BUT THERE COMES A TIME, AS IT CAME IN MY LIFE, WHEN A MAN IS DENIED THE RIGHT TO LIVE A NORMAL LIFE, WHEN HE CAN ONLY LIVE THE LIFE OF AN OUTLAW BECAUSE THE GOVERNMENT HAS SO DECREED TO USE THE LAW TO IMPOSE A STATE OF OUT-LAWRY UPON HIM. I was driven to this situation, and I do not regret having taken the decisions that I did take. Other people will be driven in the same way in this country . . ."[1]

Immediately upon going into hiding, Mandela began to organize activities for the National Action Council, an organization he headed and had helped to establish just a few days earlier. Possibly through a government oversight, his banning orders had expired near the end of the Treason Trial and had not been renewed. Four days before the verdict was handed down, he had driven to Pietermaritzburg, a town south of Johannesburg near the Indian Ocean. There, he gave the keynote address to the All-In-Africa Conference, a group of about fourteen hundred activists astonished suddenly to see their leader who had been banned for nine years.

Nelson walked onto the speaker's platform with bare feet, emphasizing that he considered himself one of the people. The onlookers loved it. The conference called for a national convention to draft a new constitution for the country, one that would regard all South Africans as equals without regard to race.

Mandela organized an election to select delegates to the National Action Council. In a unanimous vote, he was named head of the new organization. The council was given the responsibility of communicating the demands for a new constitution to the South African government. If the government did not accept the request, it was agreed, a three-day work stoppage would be held May 29, 30, and 31.

The timing of the work stoppage was significant. On May 31, 1961, dubbed "Republic Day," the Union of South Africa was scheduled to become the Republic of South Africa. The change was being made as the result of a nationwide vote but, of course, no native Africans had been asked to take part in the decision. The changeover included severing a number of ties with Great Britain and withdrawing from the Commonwealth of Nations, a number of whose members had become increasingly critical of apartheid rule. Republic Day was widely anticipated by white South Africans, but considered of little importance by most blacks. The nation-wide work stoppage was intended to show that all was not well in the brand new republic.

When it was clear to white authorities that Nelson Mandela had gone underground, a warrant was issued for his arrest. Wearing disguises, often posing as a chauffeur, Nelson moved at will throughout the nation, helped by his many supporters to avoid police capture. He urged support for the upcoming strike among workers and students.

Mandela and other National Action Council organizers went to great lengths to avoid violence during the planned three-day strike. It was decided to discourage the formation of picket lines and work-place confrontations, both common sources of violence during strikes. Instead, striking Africans were asked merely to stay at home. The plan gave little opportunity for another massacre to develop, as had happened in Sharpeville.

In letters to government officials, Mandela urged acceptance of the plan for a national convention to write a new constitution. After years of nonviolent struggle, met by increasingly violent police reactions, Nelson was obviously worried that a worse situation would soon develop. In a letter to the leader of a political party, he noted that the options were to "talk it out or shoot it out."[2]

Still, Mandela and other strike organizers hoped that the nonviolent stay-at-home would put enough economic pressure on the South African government to force a change in apartheid rules. But white officials viewed even this gentle protest as dangerous treason.

The government mobilized police and regular army forces and suspended civil liberties. Employers were told to fire all strikers. Enormous police raids descended on black townships. Print shops suspected of publishing strike calls were raided, their publications seized. By May 20, more than ten thousand Africans had been arrested, the vast majority imprisoned without trial.

"A special law had to be rushed through Parliament to enable the Government to detain without trial people connected with the organization of the stay-at-home," Nelson wrote while in hiding soon after the strike. "The Army had to be called out, European citizens armed, and the police force deployed in African townships and other areas. Meetings were banned throughout the country, and the local authorities, in collaboration with the police force, kept vigil to ensure no strike propaganda should be spread among the masses of the people. More than 10,000 innocent Africans were arrested and jailed under the pass laws and terror and intimidation became widespread."[3]

As it had so many times in the past, nonviolent protest met a violent response. But despite the government's savage effort to stop the strike, the results in some parts of the country were remarkable. On May 29, more than 60 percent of the native African work force stayed home in Johannesburg and Pretoria. In Port Elizabeth, the percentage was even higher. All of the strikers were risking the loss of their jobs, their homes, and even their freedom, or what remained of it under apartheid law.

On the next day, May 30, Nelson held a secret meeting with newspaper reporters. He explained that, considering the harsh measures taken by the government, the stay-at-home strike had been highly successful. But he also added a note of grave warning. "If the government reaction is to crush by naked force our non-violent struggle, we will have to seriously reconsider our tactics. In my mind, we are closing a chapter on this question of a non-violent policy."[4]

Living at the house in Soweto, it was difficult for Winnie to see much of her husband. But it was easy to tell where he had been most recently. Each morning, she could look at the *Rand Daily Mail* newspaper and read about Nelson's latest adventures. Always, he had made a surprise visit to this or that group, had talked, and had somehow eluded police. A number of newspaper reporters began calling him the "Black Pimpernel." The reference was to a famous fictional character, called the "Scarlet Pimpernel," who escaped capture during the French Revolution.

Assuming that Nelson would at some point try to visit his family, police watched No. 8115 in Orlando West night and day. They never found Nelson there. But Winnie did on occasion see her husband. Once, when she was driving her car in downtown Johannesburg, she pulled up to a red light and stopped. Next to her was a car driven by a man in a chauffeur's uniform. It was Nelson! Knowing that she was probably being watched by police, Winnie made no sign of recognition. Neither did her husband, who surely recognized his own car. Both drove away as soon as the light turned green.

Fortunately, Winnie had other opportunities to enjoy the company of her fugitive spouse. Many of the meetings took place at a little farmhouse, called Lilliesleaf, that a friend of Nelson's had rented in Rivonia, a suburb of Johannesburg. Winnie and her two young daughters were reunited with Nelson there often, but getting there from Soweto was a problem. In order to avoid being followed by police, Winnie and her daughters were driven in a number of different cars. To this day, she will not say exactly how the police were shaken off, fearing that the people who helped her can still be arrested.

At the Lilliesleaf farm, the Mandelas could enjoy a few moments of normal family life. Winnie cooked meals for Nelson and the children. The father held his two young daughters and took walks in a nearby orchard. But as happy as these reunions were, they were not the only purpose for the Lilliesleaf farm.

The little building was also the secret headquarters for a new organization: *Umkhonto we Sizwe*, or, in English, Spear of the Nation. In meetings with other members of the banned African National Congress, Nelson decided at last that peaceful protests were futile. After a half century of nonviolent efforts by the ANC to change the policy of South Africa's white government, conditions had only grown worse. Nelson Mandela was chosen to head a new activist group, one that was no longer limited to nonviolent protest.

With the formation of Umkhonto we Sizwe, a new and more violent era in the struggle for freedom was at hand. But Nelson showed remarkable restraint. He called for violence to be directed only at property, not people. It was important, he felt, to keep anger between the races at a minimum, so that future relations among all South Africans could be improved. He understood that full-fledged wars, especially race wars, left scars that could last for many years.

On December 16, 1961, members of Umkhonto we Sizwe struck back at the government of South Africa. In twenty-three separate acts of sabotage, all against targets selected for their symbolic importance, bombs exploded in the cities of Johannesburg, Durban, and Port Elizabeth. One person, a saboteur involved in setting up the explosives, was killed. The response of the government, which had taken insane actions when native Africans decided to remain home for three days, is easy enough to imagine.

Despite a frantic search by police, Nelson Mandela, now South Africa's most wanted man, continued to elude them.

In the early days of January 1962, he managed to slip across the country's border. It was the first time in his life he had been out of South Africa. Traveling to Addis Ababa, the capital of Ethiopia, he was reunited with his old friend Oliver Tambo. Tambo had left South Africa two years earlier, in order to establish ANC offices in other countries, where the organization had not been banned.

Addis Ababa was the site for a large Pan-African Freedom Conference hosted by the emperor of Ethiopia. Tambo made arrangements for his friend Nelson to speak at the large gathering, and the talk was extremely well received.

Together, Mandela and Tambo traveled to a number of other African nations. In many areas, they saw white and black people living together in harmony. They also traveled through nations whose governments were run by native Africans. Many of the countries they visited were extremely poor, especially by the standards of South Africa. However, they knew it was difficult to imagine how different the economy of white South Africa might be if its deposits of gold, diamonds, uranium, and other precious resources, the richest in the world, had never existed.

"Wherever I went I was treated like a human being," Mandela said. "In the African states I saw black and white mingling peacefully and happily in hotels, cinemas; trading in the same areas, using the same public transport, and living in the same residential areas."[5]

Mandela was not traveling through Africa simply as a tourist. Everywhere, he looked for places where his countrymen could be trained, as soldiers, technicians, and government leaders. More and more, he was coming to the conclusion that a war would be needed to end white supremacy in South Africa.

During his travels, he was astounded by the sense of freedom he felt. For the first time since he had been a child, he was free from apartheid laws and police harassment. It was a pleasure, he realized, to be treated like a human being.

He was free, for example, to fly to London. And so he and Oliver Tambo did just that. In the historic English city, he met leaders of two political parties and took a sightseeing trip. Then it was back to Africa, where he studied troop training and met government officials in countries that had recently won their independence from European nations.

Soon enough, he knew that he had to return to South Africa. That was where his struggle was, and where Winnie and his family were. Secretly, he slipped across the border once again. He made reports about his travels to a number of officials in the ANC and Umkhonto we Sizwe. Then he moved to a house in Johannesburg directly across from a police station, where few people would think to look for him.

South African police were now taking every step imaginable to capture the country's most wanted criminal. The head of security services for Great Britain, Sir Percy Sillitoe, was called in as a consultant. Rewards were offered for information leading to his arrest. Winnie was watched continuously. Roadblocks were established regularly on all sides of Johannesburg.

Still, sometime during the summer, Nelson and Winnie managed to meet each other at the Lilliesleaf farm. An elaborate charade was set up to move Winnie unnoticed through Johannesburg roadblocks. Carried in an ambulance, with her children and a man dressed as a doctor by her side, she pretended to be a pregnant woman in labor until she reached the safety of the Lilliesleaf farm. The visit Nelson had with his family was his last outside of prison. After seventeen months of hiding from police, his luck had finally run out.

On Sunday, August 5, 1962, three police squad cars pulled over his automobile as it was driving along a road leading to Johannesburg. The police seemed to know that Nelson was inside the car, so they must have had a tip from an informant. Nelson was promptly arrested.

He was immediately put in jail. He remained a prisoner of the South African government for 10,052 days and nights—more than twenty-seven years.

Winnie Mandela brings Nelson's mother to the court in Pretoria,
where Nelson was found guilty and sentenced to life imprisonment.

Chapter 8

THE FINAL TRIALS

Winnie first learned of her husband's arrest as she was leaving her office at the Johannesburg Child Welfare Society to do some field work in Soweto. Just as she walked off the elevator, she bumped into one of Nelson's friends.

The man looked terrible, she remembered. His face had turned white and his hair was unkempt. His clothes looked dirty and wrinkled, as if he had just gotten out of bed. As soon as she saw the man, Winnie knew that something was terribly wrong. She asked if he was all right, both knowing that the word "he" meant Nelson. The man said no, that he thought her husband would be in a Johannesburg courtroom in the morning. She knew immediately that it meant Nelson had been caught and arrested.

"It was the collapse of a political dream," she wrote later. "At that moment I wasn't only shocked for myself. I was shocked for the struggle and what it meant for the cause of my people—then, when he was at the height of his political career.

"I don't know how I reached home," she continued. "I just remember, vaguely, throwing my files in the back of my car and driving straight home. Fortunately my sister was there to console me. Of course I have since recovered from the painful shock. I knew at that time that this was the end of any kind of family life, as was the case with millions of my people—I was no exception.

"Part of my soul went with him at that time."[1]

Sitting in seats reserved for spectators, Winnie watched as her husband was led into the courtroom on August 8, 1962. It was a brief session, just to announce formal accusations. Nelson was charged with organizing the stay-at-home strike and with leaving the country without the proper papers. So far, at least, government prosecutors had no evidence linking him with the Umkhonto we Sizwe bombings. After the charges were read, the defendant was led out of the room in handcuffs.

Following several delays, the trial began in earnest on October 22, in the same Pretoria courtroom, actually an old synagogue, where the Treason Trial was held less than two years earlier. Winnie attended the sessions wearing traditional African costumes.

The court, like others throughout the country, was ultimately under the direction of South Africa's Minister of Justice, J.B.M. Vorster. During World War II, Vorster had been jailed for pro-Nazi activities. His policies seemed to indicate that he longed for the days when the Nazi soldiers of Adolf Hitler ruled much of Europe and northern Africa. Vorster found new ways to harass banned people, including prohibiting banned husbands and wives from speaking to each other. He also began house arrests, making political protesters, including Walter Sisulu, prisoners in their own homes.

A little more than a year later, the government passed a law, at Vorster's urging, allowing police to detain people in solitary confinement for up to ninety days without a trial. The wording made it legal for police to torture the people they held in order to get information from them. This, of course, was in the future. In the meantime, Vorster made it clear that it was a crime for any group of people to gather anywhere in South Africa in support of Nelson Mandela. Risking arrest, crowds of Nelson's well-wishers waited outside the Pretoria court building anyway.

Inside, the trial began. Nelson entered the room wearing an animal-skin robe, a present from his followers. Although he knew he had little chance of being found not guilty, he presented a brilliant defense nevertheless. The picture of a native African, wearing native African dress but speaking clearly and so very eloquently in English made a lasting impression on everyone present.

"I want at once to make it clear that I am no racialist," he said, "and I detest racialism, because I regard it as a barbaric thing, whether it comes from a Black man or from a White man."[2]

But he went on to say that he was forced to use the terms black and white to continue his defense.

Mandela challenged the right of the court to hear his case on two grounds. First, he felt that he would not receive a correct and fair trial. Second, he believed that he had no duty to obey laws made by a legislature in which he was not represented. He continued his defense by addressing first the question of a fair trial.

"In a political trial such as this one," he said, "which involves a clash of the aspirations of the African people and those of Whites, the country's courts, as presently constituted, cannot be impartial and fair.

"In such cases," he continued, "Whites are interested parties. To have a White judicial officer presiding, however high his esteem, and however strong his sense of fairness and justice, is to make Whites judges in their own case.

"It is improper and against the elementary principles of justice to entrust Whites with cases involving the denial by them of basic human rights to the African people."[3]

He went on to ask what kind of system of justice allowed one group of people to make a complaint against another, and then sit in judgment over them.

After an interruption by the judge, Nelson posed more questions, making points that clearly showed the essential unfairness of the trial he was about to have. "Why is it," he asked, "that in this courtroom I face a White magistrate, confronted by a White prosecutor, and escorted into the dock by a White orderly? Can anyone honestly and seriously suggest that in this type of atmosphere the scales of justice are evenly balanced?

"Why is it," he continued, "that no African in the history of this country has ever had the honour of being tried by his own kith and kin, by his own flesh and blood?"[4]

Mandela answered his own questions, explaining that South Africa's white courts were set up to carry out the policies of its white government.

Less directly, he also spoke to his second challenge, that he should not have to obey laws that neither he nor his people had any part in creating. "In their relationship with us," he said, "South African Whites regard it as fair and just to pursue policies which have outraged the conscience of mankind and of honest and upright men throughout the civilized world. They suppress our aspirations, bar our way to freedom, and deny us opportunities to promote our moral and material progress, to secure ourselves from fear and want. All the good things of life are reserved for the White folk and we Blacks are expected to be content to nourish our bodies with such pieces of food as drop from the tables of men with White skins. This is the White man's standard of justice and fairness."[5]

Despite the careful logic behind all of his statements, Mandela's challenge to the authority of the court to try him was denied. The judge then asked him how he would plead. The answer was not guilty to both charges.

Witnesses were called, examined and cross-examined, as the state made its case against Nelson. The defendant carefully questioned the secretary of South Africa's prime minister. During this questioning, he asked why the prime minister had decided not to answer a letter Nelson had written to him prior to the 1961 stay-at-home campaign. The letter gave the government leader a chance to stop the strike by agreeing to examine the question of a new constitution.

As opposed to the Treason Trial, which lasted more than four years, Nelson's new trial took just four days. On October 25, 1962, he was convicted on both counts: organizing the strike and leaving the country without permission. Sentencing was scheduled for November 7. Prior to that date, he was allowed to address the court one last time. In one of his greatest speeches, he discussed his life, the history of the South African protest movement, and his own participation in events leading up to his trial. A number of his statements quoted in earlier chapters of this book are taken from that thoughtful speech.

On November 7, the white judge sentenced Nelson Mandela to a total of five years' imprisonment with hard labor. Outside the court building, a large group of demonstrators began singing an African song called *"Tshotsholoza Mandela,"* which meant, "Carry on, Mandela."

Nelson was placed in a jail cell in Pretoria Central Prison, where he spent twenty-three hours each day in solitary confinement, ordered to sew mailbags. Soon he was transferred to Robben Island, a desolate prison colony in the Atlantic

102

Ocean near Cape Town. On Robben Island, the solitary confinement continued. His only cause for hope was the fact that, in five years, he would be set free. But even this thought was soon put in jeopardy.

Some time during 1963, police discovered the Umkhonto we Sizwe hideout. In a raid conducted at the Lilliesleaf farmhouse in Rivonia on April 11, Walter Sisulu and a number of others were captured and arrested. Sisulu had gone underground after being arrested six times the previous year and, until his capture, was hiding out at the farm once used by Nelson and Winnie. During the raid, the police discovered many documents, including some written by Nelson, that for the first time connected him with the sabotage campaign.

In all, nine people, including Mandela and Walter Sisulu, were charged with participating in a conspiracy to overthrow the government by revolution and for helping in the invasion of the country by foreign troops. Of the nine defendants, six were Africans, two were whites, and one was Indian. A possible penalty for all, once again, was death. Mandela freely admitted that he had helped organize Umkhonto we Sizwe, and so there was little chance of being found not guilty. As they had so often in the past, the defendants planned to use the trial as a platform to speak about their beliefs.

The case that became known as the Rivonia Trial began in

Pretoria's Palace of Justice on October 9, 1963. Winnie was not allowed to attend the start of her husband's trial. Her banning orders restricted her to Johannesburg. Requests to drive the short distance to Pretoria were denied.

The state presented many witnesses to discuss acts of sabotage performed by Umkhonto we Sizwe. At least a few of the witnesses were shown to be liars. However, considerable evidence existed indicating that Nelson and some of the other defendants had planned sabotage. The state took five months to present its case, finally resting on February 29, 1964. More than a month would pass before the defense began.

Court was back in session on April 20. This time, Winnie was able to attend, as was Nelson's mother, who traveled from the Transkei to Pretoria to see her son's defense. She told Winnie that she was very proud of him.

Even though the defendants were on trial for their lives, Nelson never even considered lying in court in an attempt to save himself. Although he had pleaded not guilty, he freely admitted to planning a number of bombings. At the same time, however, he and the others wanted to set the record straight, to correct some misstatements made by the prosecution. They made it clear, for example, that although preparations for war were being made, everyone involved in Umkhonto we Sizwe still hoped to avoid it and had made no specific battle plans.

Soon after court was back in session, Nelson rose to his feet as the first witness for the defense. He refused to be cross-examined, but, wearing glasses to make the task easier, read out loud a long statement he had written earlier. Near the beginning, he pointed out that some of the things said in court so far had been true, others untrue.

"I do not, however, deny that I planned sabotage," he continued. "I did not plan it in a spirit of recklessness, nor because I have any love of violence. I planned it as a result of a calm and sober assessment of the political situation that had arisen after many years of tyranny, exploitation, and oppression of my people by the Whites.

"I admit immediately that I was one of the persons who helped to form Umkhonto we Sizwe, and that I played a prominent role in its affairs until I was arrested in August 1962."[6]

The results of the Rivonia Trial, announced June 12, 1964, were a foregone conclusion. After all, government officials announced before the trial began that the defendants were guilty. Of the nine men charged, eight, including Nelson and Walter Sisulu, were sentenced to life imprisonment. The ninth defendant was found not guilty and promptly rearrested on another charge. Some people considered the judgment lenient, since the death penalty could have been called for.

Much of the world directed harsh criticism at the South

African government. *The New York Times* called Mandela and the other defendants the George Washingtons and Ben Franklins of South Africa. But there was little time for the African patriots to consider world opinion. As soon as the judge announced the life sentences, the defendants looked at the courtroom spectators and smiled. Nelson stuck his thumb up in the air, for years the symbol of the African National Congress.

The prisoners were led away, to be taken to Robben Island where Nelson would spend the next twenty years. Winnie hurried to the street in front of the courtroom. There she held her two young daughters and hoped for one last glimpse of Nelson. But the large crowd, made up mostly of Africans singing freedom songs and dancing, was too large.

In a moment, someone grabbed Winnie's shoulder. It was a big South African policeman. "Remember your permit!" he ordered Winnie. "You must be back in Johannesburg by twelve o'clock!"[7]

Chapter 9

PRISONER OF CONSCIENCE

On the night of June 13, 1964, Nelson Mandela, Walter Sisulu, and the six other men convicted in the Rivonia Trial were flown to Cape Town. From there, they were taken on a ferryboat to the maximum security prison on Robben Island, where each man began serving his life sentence.

The first task given the new inmates was to build their own jail cells, specially designed to isolate them from the rest of the prisoners. One of the rough guards who watched over their toil wore a Nazi swastika on the back of his hand.

By the time he moved into his tiny cell, each wall about seven feet long, Nelson Mandela had reached his forty-sixth birthday. For a time, he was forced to stay in the enclosure constantly. Three tiny and wretched meals were served each day. On Saturdays, prison officials listened to complaints from prisoners, often laughing. But Mandela made serious demands anyway, eventually winning tiny concessions.

First, the prisoners were allowed to go outside in the prison yard, where they broke up rocks with hammers. They were not allowed to talk to one another, but whispered together anyway. Those who were caught were forced to go without three meals. Later, the prisoners were marched, in chains, to a stone quarry, a deep hole in the ground, where they continued to break up rocks.

In August, Winnie was allowed a visit with her husband on Robben Island. Arrangements were difficult, because she not only had to negotiate with prison authorities, but, because of her banning orders, also with local police as well as government bureaucrats. In the Robben Island visiting room, a glass wall stood between the prisoners and their visitors. Winnie had to speak with her husband on a telephone, only able to see him through the thick glass.

Even under these harsh circumstances, husband and wife were prohibited from talking about anything except family matters. To make sure that instructions were being followed, guards listened in on the conversation. Even a tape recording was made. When she returned home, Winnie found that her house had been searched by police. The mess inside was astounding.

As far as the South African government was concerned, Nelson Mandela no longer existed. But now that he was imprisoned for life, the government's fury descended on Winnie and her children. Police watched the house, No. 8115 in Orlando West, night and day. They often followed Winnie when she left her home. When a friend took Zeni and Zindzi, as the Mandela's two girls were called, to a school reserved for people of mixed races, she was promptly arrested. Winnie had only wanted them to enjoy the slightly higher standards of instruction allowed in those kinds of schools.

Not much later, her banning orders were made even more

strict. Now, she was not permitted to enter any black township in Soweto except Orlando West, her own. With these new restrictions, it was impossible to perform her duties as a social worker. Tearfully, the director of the Child Welfare Society told Winnie that she would have to leave. "But you are not being fired—" she added, "if your banning order is relaxed we will take you back."[1]

But her orders were not eased. She was forced to take low-paying jobs usually filled by unskilled workers, in a furniture shop and then a dry cleaner. But the police forced her employers to fire her. Occasionally, she was able to get better jobs, once at a correspondence school for black reporters, another time as an assistant to a lawyer. In both instances, the police forced her to give up the work. Only the help of friends enabled her to live. Friends also helped her send Zeni and Zindzi to boarding school to escape police harassment.

Finally, in May 1969, nearly five years after Nelson was sent to Robben Island, her struggle to exist in her Soweto home came to an end. She and twenty-one others were arrested and charged with trying to reestablish the African National Congress. She was jailed in solitary confinement for nine months, fed disgusting food that resulted in severe malnutrition, and was sometimes questioned for days without being allowed to sleep. Eventually, she was offered freedom if she called on ANC members to resign. She refused, and the long days and nights of imprisonment continued.

Nine months after she was arrested, without a trial, she was finally brought to a courtroom. There, the charges were dropped and new ones immediately made. These too were eventually dropped, but not until she had spent 491 days, nearly a year and a half, in jail, most of that time in solitary confinement. Two weeks after her release, she was placed under house arrest at night and on weekends.

From his tiny prison cell on Robben Island, Nelson was powerless to help his wife in her struggles. But through work slowdowns, hunger strikes, and other demonstrations, he and his fellow inmates were able to attract worldwide attention. Eventually, prison officials were forced to provide somewhat better conditions. Inmates were at last allowed to talk to one another, food was improved slightly, and warmer clothing was supplied during the cold winter months. Eventually, prisoners were allowed to study textbooks, read newspapers, and grow their own vegetables in little gardens.

Late in 1973 came an offer from the minister of prisons that none of the inhabitants of Robben Island expected. The South African government was in the process of setting up a number of reserves, which it called "homelands," for African natives. In time, the government would regard each of these homelands as independent nations, a claim recognized by no other country on earth. The government would also strip many blacks of their South African citizenship and force them to live in one of the new zones. One of these so-called independent areas was the Transkei, where both Nelson and Winnie Mandela were born.

The minister of prisons offered to cancel the life sentences imposed on Nelson and a number of his fellow prisoners if they would recognize the independence of the Transkei and agree to live there. It is difficult to imagine a prisoner serving a life sentence turning down such an offer. But Nelson Mandela and those around him did just that. The total areas offered as homelands by the South African government were small and the land of little consequence to the rich economy of the nation. Although the offer was repeated on several occasions, Nelson and the other prisoners always turned it down.

Accused of breaking her bans, Winnie was again forced to serve a prison term in 1974, shortly after her husband decided not to cooperate with the government. The term lasted six months. Three years later, she received another harsh sentence.

At about 4 A.M. on the night of May 16, 1977, more than twenty policemen surrounded No. 8115 in Orlando West. All at once, the men began banging on the doors, windows, and walls. Inside, Winnie and her daughter Zindzi, now sixteen years old, were sleeping. Zeni was away. As soon as she was awakened by the racket, Winnie realized that it was another arrest. She always kept a packed suitcase by the front door for just such emergencies. But soon she understood that this arrest was different.

After hours of interrogation, the mother and daughter were placed in an army truck, along with all of their household furniture and belongings, and driven to a police station in the faraway town of Brandfort. From there, they were taken to a tiny three-room house filled with dirt and garbage. Winnie had been banished to an area where most people spoke not English but Afrikaans, a language she really had never learned. None of her old furniture would fit through the tiny door of her new home, so it was taken back to the police station.

Winnie lived in the Brandfort house during the years 1977 to 1985, leaving the area only on rare occasions to visit her husband in prison. During most of that time, she was under house arrest at night and on weekends, and was forbidden to have visitors. She returned to Soweto in 1985, after the Brandfort house was bombed and burned.

Despite the fact that so many political leaders had been killed, imprisoned, and banished, unrest and violence continued to plague South Africa. No one seemed immune from police retaliations. On June 16, 1976, young schoolchildren in Soweto marched along the street to protest the teaching of Afrikaans in the schools. A number of students, including a thirteen-year-old child, were shot dead by police.

Months of school boycotts and riots followed. Hundreds of

people were killed, thousands vanished into police custody. Soon it was discovered that a number of police captives, mostly notably including a man named Steven Biko, had died while in jail. In Biko's case, his death almost certainly was the result of torture by police. In the months and years that followed, confrontations became even more violent. In 1979, guerrilla fighters began attacking government police stations in black townships. Several policemen were killed. More peaceful forms of protest also continued.

"Release Mandela" became a rallying cry of South African protest. In January 1980, three gunmen in a Pretoria bank took twenty-five hostages in an unsuccessful attempt to gain Mandela's release, an action Nelson would have certainly criticized.

A "Free Mandela" campaign launched at Witwatersrand University two months later resulted in fifty-eight thousand signatures on a petition and widespread international support. In June of the same year, the Security Council of the United Nations called on the South African government to release Mandela and other political prisoners. Lines of graffiti, such as "Release Mandela Now" and "Nelson Lives!" were common throughout the country, especially in black townships.

On April 1, 1982, Mandela and five other prisoners were removed from Robben Island under great secrecy and moved to Pollsmoor Prison, a maximum security facility on the African mainland near Cape Town. The move was probably made to stop Nelson's efforts at organizing the other Robben Island prisoners in campaigns for better living and working conditions.

During the weekend of May 12 and 13, 1984, Winnie and Zeni, now with her own child (making Winnie a grandmother), were allowed a contact visit with Nelson. "Can you imagine!" Winnie wrote. "We last touched his hand in 1962. . . . We kissed Nelson and held him a long time. It is an experience one just can't put into words. It was fantastic and hurting at the same time."[2]

The government repeated its offer to free Mandela and others if they would move to the Transkei and support the plan for independent native homelands. Once again, Nelson refused, giving up an opportunity for freedom to avoid endorsing the government's resettlement plan.

Realizing that Mandela was becoming a martyr and a symbol of black resistance to white supremacy, South African officials continued to search for ways to release him. Soon, they dropped their demands for him to move to the Transkei and to support the idea of native African homelands.

At the end of January 1985, South African president P.W. Botha unveiled the latest plan to the South African legislature. In his speech, Botha said that Mandela could be released if he would give up planning and executing acts of violence for political purposes. "It is therefore not the South African government which now stands in the way of Mr. Mandela's freedom," Botha said. "It is he himself. The choice is his. All that is required of him now is that he should unconditionally reject violence as a political instrument. This is, after all, a norm which is respected in all civilized countries of the world."[3]

It was a highly unusual speech. The president of a wealthy and powerful nation was almost begging a prisoner to accept a simple condition for release. By this time, Nelson had spent the last twenty-three years in prison. He was sixty-six years old.

Many times in the past, he had written heartfelt letters to South African leaders. Those letters had been ignored, at best passed on to assistants and lesser bureaucrats for answers. Now, Nelson felt little need to answer President Botha directly.

About a week after the South African president made his offer, Winnie and an attorney traveled to Pollsmoor Prison to get Nelson's reply to Botha's offer. It was decided to let Zindzi read her father's statement directly to the South African people.

An ideal opportunity arose on Sunday, February 10. On that date, a large meeting was held in Soweto's Jabulani Stadium to celebrate the winning by South African Anglican Bishop Desmond Tutu of the Nobel Peace Prize. It was the second time that a native African active in the country's protest movement had won the famous award.

When the day came, Zindziswa Mandela read her father's reply. The speech Mandela wrote included references to other white South African leaders in addition to Botha, including Malan, Strijdom, and Verwoerd.

"I am surprised at the conditions that the Government wants to impose on me," Zindzi read for her father. "I am not a violent man. My colleagues and I wrote in 1952 to Malan asking for a round-table conference to find a solution to the problems of our country but that was ignored.

"When Strijdom was in power, we made the same offer. Again it was ignored. When Verwoerd was in power we asked for a national convention for all the people in South Africa to decide on their own future. This, too, was in vain.

"It was only then when all other forms of resistance were no longer open to us that we turned to armed struggle.

"Let Botha show that he is different to Malan, Strijdom and Verwoerd.

"Let him renounce violence.

"Let him say that he will dismantle apartheid.

"Let him unban the people's organization, the African National Congress.

"Let him free all who have been imprisoned, banished or exiled for their opposition to apartheid.

"Let him guarantee free political activity so that the people may decide who will govern them.

"I cherish my own freedom dearly but I care even more for your freedom. Too many have died since I went to prison. Too many have suffered for the love of freedom. I owe it to their widows, to their orphans, to their mothers and to their fathers who have grieved and wept for them. Not only I have suffered during these long, lonely, wasted years.

"I am not less life-loving than you are. But I cannot sell my birthright, nor am I prepared to sell the birthright of the people to be free. I am in prison as the representative of the people and of your organization, the African National Congress, which was banned. What freedom am I being offered while the organization of the people remains banned? What freedom am I being offered when I may be arrested on a pass offence? What freedom am I being offered to live my life as a family with my dear wife who remains in banishment in Brandfort? What freedom am I being offered when I must ask for permission to live in an urban area? What freedom am I being offered when I need a stamp in my pass to seek work? What freedom am I being offered when my very South African citizenship is not respected? Only free men can negotiate. Prisoners cannot enter into contracts.

"I cannot and will not give any undertaking at a time when I and you the people are not free. Your freedom and mine cannot be separated. I will return."[4]

Millions of South Africans hoped that Nelson Mandela

would someday return to the outside world. But his answer to Botha's offer was clear, and so he remained in prison.

Throughout his life, Nelson was strong and athletic. He exercised every day, even when he was locked alone in a tiny jail cell. During much of his prison life, he grew vegetables in tiny gardens in order to improve his diet.

But in 1988, he contracted tuberculosis. Family friends and a doctor stated that this was undoubtedly caused by conditions in his prison cell. In December, after Nelson was declared cured of tuberculosis, he was moved to a guarded house on Verster Prison Farm. He, like many other African protest leaders, had given up his freedom and endangered his health for a struggling people.

In 1989, Winnie Mandela was the subject of disturbing newspaper reports. A group of about thirty youths, called the "United Mandela Football Club," had been organized to protect her. Unfortunately, the undisciplined bodyguards reportedly terrorized many people in Soweto. Winnie followed her husband's advice to disband the group.

Far happier news was made about a year later. Under worldwide pressure, South African president F.W. deKlerk decided to release Nelson Mandela. On Sunday, February 11, 1990, Nelson walked out of Verster Prison with Winnie at his side. Although he was now seventy-one years old, he appeared trim and strong, walking like a man half his age.

Nelson traveled by car to nearby Cape Town. At city hall,

thousands of people had gathered to hear him speak for the first time in nearly thirty years. A few members of the crowd became unruly and broke store windows. Some were shot at close range by police. Order was only restored when Mandela arrived.

Under bright television lights set up on the steps of city hall, Nelson began reading his speech. "I greet you all in the name of peace, democracy and freedom for all," he said. He added that some progress in race relations had been made in South Africa, but that many problems remained. "The factors which necessitated the armed struggle still exist today," he said. He concluded his speech by quoting his own words from his trial in 1964.

"I have fought against white domination and I have fought against black domination," he said. "I have cherished the ideal of a democratic and free society in which all persons live together in harmony and with equal opportunity. It is an ideal which I hope to live for and to achieve. But if need be, it is an idea for which I am prepared to die."

Within a matter of days, the white South African government announced plans to hold a series of meetings with black South African leaders. Perhaps the conference would lead to a new constitution for the nation. At long, long last, there seemed to be a faint glimmer of hope spreading over the South African sky.

A child lies on a mattress while his parents salvage possessions from their blazing shack in Cape Town's squatter camp in January 1988. After two nights of battles in the camp, five people were reported dead and fifteen hundred homeless.

Nelson Mandela 1918-

1918 Nelson Mandela is born in the Transkei. World War I armistice is signed between Allies and Germany on November 11. President Woodrow Wilson arrives in Paris for peace conference. Daylight savings time is introduced in the U.S. The first airmail service is established between New York City and Washington, D.C. The true dimensions of the Milky Way are discovered.

1919 The Prohibition Amendment (18th) to the U.S. constitution is ratified. President Wilson presides over the first League of Nations meeting in Paris. Jan Smuts succeeds Louis Botha as prime minister of the Union of South Africa. First experiments are carried out with shortwave radio. Ross Macpherson and Keith Smith fly from London to Australia in 135 hours. Babe Ruth hits a 587-foot home run in a New York Giants game against the Boston Red Sox.

1920 The League of Nations gives South Africa control of Namibia. In the U.S., the Nineteenth Amendment gives women the vote. Warren G. Harding is elected president of the U.S. Guglielmo Marconi opens the first public broadcasting station in Britain. The sport of waterskiing is pioneered in France.

1921 Adolf Hitler's storm troopers begin to terrorize political opponents. Albert Einstein wins the Nobel prize for physics. The first radio broadcast of a baseball game is made from the Polo Grounds in New York. The old game of table tennis is revived. The Unknown Soldier is interred at Arlington National Cemetery near Washington, D.C. Ku Klux Klan activities become violent throughout the southern U.S. destroying property and whipping blacks and their sympathizers.

1922 The League of Nations council approves mandates for Palestine and Egypt. Benito Mussolini forms fascist government in Italy. One of the world's greatest volcanoes is discovered on the Alaskan Coast. A self-winding wristwatch is patented in the U.S. A tennis stadium is opened at Wimbledon outside of London.

1923 Lee de Forest demonstrates a process for sound motion pictures. German designer Willy Messerschmitt establishes his aircraft factory. The first crossing of the English Channel from France to England is achieved by an Argentine swimmer, Enrique Triboschi.

1924 In addition to English, Afrikaans becomes the official language in South Africa. The World Chess League is founded at The Hague, the Netherlands. Insecticides are used for the first time. Danish polar explorer Knud Rasmussen completes the longest dog-sled journey ever made across the North American Arctic. The first Winter Olympics are held.

1925 Hitler reorganizes the Nazi Party and writes *Mein Kampf*. The first International Congress of Radiologists is held in London. Crossword puzzles become fashionable. John T. Scopes, a schoolteacher, goes on trail for violating Tennessee law that prohibits teaching the theory of evolution.

1926 Germany is admitted into the League of Nations. The George Washington Bridge is planned to span the Hudson River between New Jersey and New York. Kodak produces the first 16-mm movie film. The permanent wave is invented.

1927 Charles Lindbergh flies the *Spirit of St. Louis* nonstop from New York to Paris in 33.5 hours. Babe Ruth hits 60 home runs for the New York Yankees.

1928 Herbert Hoover is elected president of the U.S. John L. Baird demonstrates color TV. Alexander Fleming discovers penicillin. The first color motion pictures are exhibited by George Eastman in Rochester, New York.

1929 The stock-market crash in the U.S. triggers a worldwide depression. The term "apartheid" is used for the first time. Admiral Richard Byrd and three companions fly over the South Pole. American manufacturers begin to make aluminum furniture. Kodak introduces 16-mm color movie film. St. Valentine's Day Massacre; six notorious Chicago gangsters are gunned down by a rival gang. Lieutenant James Doolittle pilots a plane solely with instruments.

1930 Nelson Mandela's dying father sends him to live with the chief of Thembu. Contract bridge gains popularity in the U.S. as a card game. Comic strips gain in popularity. The photoflash bulb comes into use. South African microbiologist Max Theiler invents a yellow fever vaccine.

1931 Great Britain gives South Africa full independence as a member of the Commonwealth of Nations. Australian explorer G.H. Wilkins captains the *Nautilus* submarine. Hattie T. Caraway becomes the first woman to be elected to the U.S. Senate.

1932 Franklin D. Roosevelt wins the U.S. presidency in a landslide. Austrian-born Adolf Hitler receives German citizenship. Amelia Earhardt is the first woman to fly solo across the Atlantic. Japan begins its conquest of world markets by cutting prices. Auguste Piccard reaches a height of 17.5 miles in a balloon.

1933 U.S. Congress votes independence for the Philippines. Hitler is appointed chancellor of Germany. Philo Farnsworth develops electronic television. The first all-star baseball game is played. Prohibition is repealed in the U.S. (21st Amendment). The U.S. recognizes the U.S.S.R.

1934 Hitler and Mussolini meet in Venice, Italy. Hitler becomes furher of Germany. U.S.S.R. is admitted to the League of Nations. The Dionne quintuplets are born in Canada. The F.B.I. shoots John Dillinger, "Public Enemy, No. 1."

1935 Roosevelt signs the U.S. Social Security Act. Chiang Kai-shek becomes president of China. Radar equipment to detect aircraft is built. The longest bridge in the world opens over the lower Zambesi in Africa. The Curies (Marie and Pierre) receive the Nobel prize for the synthesis of new radioactive elements. The S.S. *Normandie* crosses the Atlantic in 107 hours and 33 minutes.

1936 Winnie Mandela is born. The Representation of Natives Act and the Native Trust and Land Act are passed in South Africa, limiting the freedoms of blacks. German troops occupy the Rhineland; Hitler wins 99 percent of the vote. The Spanish Civil War begins. F.D. Roosevelt is reelected by a landslide.

1937 George VI is crowned king of Great Britain. Italy withdraws from the League of Nations. The Lincoln Tunnel is opened between New York and New Jersey. The Golden Gate Bridge opens in San Francisco. Amelia Earhardt vanishes while attempting a round-the-world flight.

1938 Nelson Mandela begins his college studies. Hitler appoints himself war minister. Prime Minister Winston Churchill leads British outcry against Hitler. U.S. Supreme Court rules that University of Missouri Law School must admit blacks because of lack of other facilities in the area. The ballpoint pen is invented in Hungary.

1939 Roosevelt asks Congress for $552 million for defense. Spanish Civil War ends. Britain and France recognize Franco's government in Spain. Germany invades Poland. Britain and France declare war on Germany. The first baseball game is televised in the U.S. Pan-American Airlines begins regularly scheduled flights between U.S. and Europe.

1940 Mandela joins a strike and is suspended from college. Germany invades Norway and Denmark. Belgium capitulates to Germany. Roosevelt is elected to a third term. The first electron microscope is demonstrated. The first successful helicopter flight takes place in the U.S.

1941 Mandela goes to Johannesburg and studies law. Japan attacks the U.S. at Pearl Harbor. U.S. and Britain declare war on Japan. Germany and Italy declare war on the U.S. U.S. declares war on Germany and Italy. The Manhattan Project of intense atomic research begins in Chicago.

1942 World War II rages on two fronts. The murder of millions of Jews in Nazi gas chambers begins. The first automatic computer is developed in the U.S. The first bowling tournament is held in the U.S.

1943 World War II continues. U.S. forces regain islands in the Pacific. Allies invade Italy. Penicillin issued successfully in the treatment of chronic diseases. Infantile paralysis (polio) epidemic kills about 1,200 in U.S. and cripples more. Race riots break out in several U.S. cities whose labor forces face competition from influx of southern blacks.

1944 American troops land in Normandy, France. Roosevelt is elected for a fourth term. The first plane flies nonstop from London to Canada.

1945 Roosevelt and Joseph Stalin of the U.S.S.R. meet at Yalta. Roosevelt dies and is succeeded by Harry Truman. Hitler commits suicide. The war in Europe ends. The first atomic bomb is detonated in New Mexico. U.S. drops atomic bomb on Hiroshima and Nagasaki. Japan surrenders. The Arab League is founded to oppose creation of the Jewish state.

1946 The UN General Assembly holds its first meeting in London, England. The Nuremburg tribunal finds Ribbentrop, Goering, and ten other Nazis guilty; they are sentenced to death. Xerography process is invented.

1947 The British proposal to divide Palestine is rejected by Arabs and Jews. The question is referred to the UN, which announces plans for partition. India is proclaimed independent. The first U.S. airplane flies at supersonic speeds. Jackie Robinson becomes the first black to sign a contract with a major baseball club.

1948 The National party is formed by the Afrikaners; it is dedicated to apartheid. In South Africa the area of Soweto is founded. The Jewish State of Israel is born.

1949 Chiang Kai-shek resigns as president of China; the Communist People's Republic is proclaimed. Israel is admitted to the UN. A Democratic Republic is established in East Germany. The U.S.S.R. tests its first atomic bomb. A U.S. air force jet flies across the U.S. in 3 hours and 46 minutes.

1950 There is a nationwide work stoppage in South Africa. Mandela becomes president of the African National Congress (ANC) Youth League and appeals to everyone opposed to apartheid. Britain recognizes Communist China. Senator Joseph McCarthy, from Wisconsin, advises President Truman that the State Department is riddled with Communists and Communist sympathizers. There are riots in Johannesburg against apartheid. Britain recognizes Israel. Antihistamines become a popular remedy for colds and allergies.

1951 Charles Blair flies solo over the North Pole. Color TV is introduced in the U.S. A heart-lung machine is devised for heart operations.

1952 In South Africa there are protests against apartheid. Nelson Mandela is arrested for defying 11:00 P.M. curfew; he is given a suspended sentence, however. He opens a law office in partnership with Oliver Tambo. Anti-British riots erupt in Egypt. Queen Elizabeth II comes to the British throne. Dwight D. Eisenhower is elected president of the U.S.

1953 Mandela appears in court as a lawyer. ANC members go underground. Winnie Mandela moves to Johannesburg. Lung cancer is attributed to smoking. Edmund Hillary and Norgay Tenzing are the first to climb Mt. Everest.

1954 Attempts to disbar Mandela are unsuccessful. The U.S. Supreme Court rules that segregation by color in public schools is a violation of the 14th Amendment. U.S. and Canada agree to build radar warning stations across northern Canada (DEW line). The U.S. submarine *Nautilus* is converted to nuclear power.

1955 Winnie Mandela becomes the first black medical social worker in South Africa. Blacks in Montgomery, Alabama, boycott segregated bus lines. Commercial TV begins broadcasting in Britain.

1956 Nelson Mandela is arrested and charged with being a Communist conspirator. Gamal Abdel Nasser is elected president of Egypt. Eisenhower is reelected president of the U.S. Martin Luther King, Jr. emerges as leader of the campaign for desegregation in the U.S. The oral vaccine against polio is developed by Alfred Sabin.

1957 U.S.S.R. launches *Sputnik I* and *II*, the first earth satellites. There is a desegregation crisis in Little Rock, Arkansas. Eisenhower dispatches paratroopers to forestall violence.

1958 Nelson and Winnie Mandela are married and move to No. 8115 in Soweto, then called Orlando West. Winnie arrested and jailed for 1 month. The European Common Market comes into being. Tension grows in the U.S. as desegregation of schools is attempted. U.S. launches a first moon rocket; it fails to reach the moon. Alaska becomes the 49th state.

1959 Nelson and Winnie Mandela's first daughter is born. The Pan African Congress (PAC) is formed. Hawaii becomes the 50th U.S. state. Louis Leakey finds the skull of man in Tanganyika (dated about 600,000 B.C.).

1960 The Sharpeville massacre; 69 killed and almost 200 wounded. Almost 2,000 political leaders imprisoned. Mandela is imprisoned through the spring and summer. John F. Kennedy is elected president of the U.S. The American Heart Association reports that smoking causes higher death rates from heart disease.

1961 The Republic of South Africa is born. Nelson Mandela goes into hiding and works for freedom causes. There is a work stoppage in May and sabotage acts against the government on December 16. White and black liberals in the U.S. loosely organize "Freedom Riders" to test and force integration in the South.

1962 Nelson Mandela leaves South Africa and travels to other areas to get support. When he sneaks back into South Africa he is arrested and is put on trial. Mandela defends himself, but is convicted and sentenced to 5 years of hard labor. A U.S. military council is established in Vietnam. James Meredith, a black applicant, is denied admission to the University of Mississippi by the governor. U.S. marshals intervene.

1963 The Rivonia Trial takes place in South Africa; 9 people, including Mandela, are tried for conspiracy. Riots and beatings by whites and police mark civil-rights struggles. President Kennedy is assassinated and Lyndon B. Johnson becomes president.

1964 Rivonia Trial ends and Nelson Mandela is sentenced to life imprisonment. Winnie is again arrested and then released. Lyndon Johnson is elected president. The poll tax is abolished in the U.S. by the 24th Amendment.

1965 There are outbreaks of violence in Selma, Alabama. Martin Luther King, Jr. heads procession of 4,000 civil-rights demonstrators from Selma to Montgomery. Students demonstrate in Washington, D.C. against U.S. involvement in war in Vietnam.

1966 Six-Day War between Israel and Arab nations ends in Israeli victory; Jerusalem proclaimed united city under Israeli rule. First human heart-transplant operation performed in Cape Town, South Africa, by Dr. Christiaan Barnard. Fifty thousand persons demonstrate against Vietnam War at Lincoln Memorial in Washington, D.C.

1968 Martin Luther King Jr. is assassinated in Memphis, Tennessee. Senator Robert F. Kennedy is assassinated in Los Angeles immediately after winning California Democratic presidential primary. Richard Nixon is elected president of the U.S.

1969 Winnie arrested again, spends many months in jail, and is finally released under house arrest. Many protests against American involvement in Vietnam. Representatives of 39 nations meet in Rome to survey pollution of the seas.

1970 Student protests against Vietnam War result in killing of four by the National Guard at Kent State University in Ohio. In France and Britain nuclear-powered pacemakers are implanted in three patients.

1971 The International Court of Justice declares South Africa's control of Namibia illegal. U.S. planes bomb Vietcong supply routes in Cambodia. U.S. conducts large-scale bombing raids against North Vietnam. Amtrak begins to operate U.S. passenger trains.

1972 District of Columbia police arrest 5 men inside Democratic National Headquarters at the Watergate complex—beginning the Watergate affair. Richard Nixon reelected president. *Apollo 16* astronauts spend 71 hours on the surface of the moon. Arab terrorists kill two Israeli Olympic athletes in Munich.

1973 Five out of seven Watergate defendants plead guilty. Four persons high up in the Nixon administration resign as a result of Watergate revelations. Vietnam peace pacts signed in Paris.

1974 Winnie Mandela serves another 6 months in jail. Impeachment hearings against Richard Nixon begin. Nixon resigns. Gerald Ford is sworn in as president.

1975 U.S. forces are evacuated from Saigon as Communist forces complete takeover of South Vietnam.

1976 Blacks riot in Soweto, beginning unrest that still continues. U.S. celebrates its Bicentennial.

1977 Winnie banished from Soweto, goes to Brandfort to live. President Jimmy Carter pardons most Vietnam draft evaders who numbered some 10,000. A new Energy Department is established.

1978 U.S. Senate votes to turn over the Panama Canal to Panama in 1999. House Select Committee on Assassinations opens hearings into assassinations of President Kennedy and Martin Luther King, Jr. The committee concluded that conspiracies were likely in both cases, but there was no hard evidence for future prosecutions.

1979 A major accident occurs at a nuclear reactor at Three Mile Island near Middletown, Pennsylvania. Sixty-three Americans are taken hostage at the American Embassy in Teheran.

1980 "Release Mandela" becomes a rallying cry. Ronald Reagan is elected president of the U.S. Eight Americans are killed and 5 wounded in an ill-fated attempt to rescue the American hostages in Teheran.

1981 Moments after the inauguration of President Reagan, the American hostages are released. Sandra Day O'Connor becomes the first woman member of the U.S. Supreme Court.

1982 The U.S. Senate votes in favor of a bill that virtually eliminated busing for the purposes of racial integration. A retired dentist, Barney Clark, becomes the first recipient of a permanent artificial heart.

1983 Sally Ride becomes the first American woman to travel in space. U.S. Marines and a small force from 6 Caribbean nations invade the island of Grenada to protect the lives of 1,000 U.S. citizens on the island. The operation is successful.

1984 South Africa adopts a new constitution; opposition forms under the United Democratic front. President Reagan is reelected.

1985 Brandfort house where Winnie is living is bombed and burned. Winnie returns to Soweto.

Reagan announces a major program to send wheat and other foodstuffs to Ethiopia and other African countries that had suffered from severe drought.

1986   South African government announces that passbooks for blacks are eliminated, allowing them to move freely. The tenth anniversary of the Soweto protest is observed; the government imposes press sanctions and blacks stage large-scale work stoppages.

1987   Civil rights law of 1966 reaffirmed and broadened by U.S. Supreme Court. Russian leader Mikhail Gorbachev visits the U.S.

1988   The government announces that Mandela has tuberculosis and he is placed in a private clinic. South Africa's ultra-right Conservative party, seeking further restrictions on blacks, gains strength in Transvaal elections. George Bush is elected president of the U.S. In December, Mandela is transferred to a guarded house on Verster Prison Farm. His family is given "unlimited access," but Winnie rejects this. She says she will take no more than the usual 40-minute visits until all political prisoners get the same privileges.

1989   In January and February, controversy arose over allegedly violent activities directed against black youths by the "United Mandela Football Club," a group of young natives organized to guard Winnie Mandela. From prison, Nelson called for the group to disband. At about the same time, approximately three hundred antiapartheid inmates in South African prisons began a life-threatening hunger strike. "The Revolutionary climate is still very high," said a white government spokesman, adding that the hunger strike would be futile. During the third week, however, the government announced it would immediately release hundreds of prisoners if the hunger strike ended. In the first two weeks after the strike was called off, the government freed three hundred of the approximately eight hundred prisoners held without trial under emergency laws. The National party wins a general election and F.W. deKlerk becomes president on September 20. DeKlerk frees from prison some antiapartheid leaders, including Walter Sisulu, a colleague of Nelson Mandela.

1990   Nelson Mandela is freed after spending more than 27 years in prison. The Separate Amenities Act, mandating segregation in public areas, is repealed. The African National Congress suspends its advocacy of armed struggle to end apartheid (with conditions). DeKlerk legalizes the African National Congress, the Pan Africanist Congress, and the South African Communist Party.

1991   The Population Registration Act, which classifies a person by race at birth, is repealed. DeKlerk, Mandela, and other political leaders pledge to end civil violence. Rajiv Gandhi, India's prime minister, is assassinated. Aung San Suu Kyi of Burma receives the Nobel Peace Prize. The U.S.S.R. faces radical change: eleven former Soviet republics form the Commonwealth of Independent States.

1992   DeKlerk calls a referendum of whites to vote for his policies of change; the referendum wins by 68.7 percent of the voters. Multiparty talks with deKlerk, Mandela, and Mangosuthu Buthelezi, leader of the Inkatha Freedom party break off. Rigoberta Menchú, a Quické Indian from Guatamala, receives the Nobel Peace Prize for her work for human rights.

1993   Talks including African National Congress, the National party, the Conservative party, the Pan Africanist Congress, and other groups resume in March.

ACKNOWLEDGMENTS

The editors would like to acknowledge use of excerpted material from the following works:

No Easy Walk to Freedom by Nelson Mandela. Copyright © 1956 by Nelson Mandela. Published by Heinemann Educational Books Ltd. Used by permission.

Reprinted from NELSON MANDELA, The Man and the Movement, by Mary Benson, by permission of Penguin Books and W.W. Norton & Company, Inc. Copyright © by Mary Benson.

Reprinted from PART OF MY SOUL WENT WITH HIM by Winnie Mandela, Edited by Anne Benjamin and Adapted by Mary Benson, by permission of Penguin Books and W.W. Norton & Company, Inc. Copyright © by Rowahlt Taschenbush Verlag GmbH, Reinbeck bei Hamburg.

Reprinted from WINNIE MANDELA by Nancy Harrison with permission of Victor Gollance Ltd. and (USA Edition) with permission of George Braziller, Publishers. © 1985 by Nancy Harrison. All rights reserved.

NOTES

Chapter 2
1. Nelson Mandela, *No Easy Walk to Freedom* (Oxford: Heinemann Educational Books Ltd., 1965): 147
2. Ibid., 147-48
3. Mary Benson, *Nelson Mandela, the Man and the Movement* (London: Penguin Books: New York: W.W. Norton & Company, 1986): 17

Chapter 3
1. Mandela, *No Easy Walk to Freedom*, x
2. Benson, *Nelson Mandela, the Man and the Movement*, 21
3. Mandela, *No Easy Walk to Freedom*, 21

Chapter 4
1. Benson, *Nelson Mandela, the Man and the Movement*, 39
2. Mandela, *No Easy Walk to Freedom*, 83
3. Ibid., 21
4. Ibid., 150-51

Chapter 5
1. Mandela, *No Easy Walk to Freedom*, ix
2. Ibid., xii
3. Ibid., 149
4. *Liberation*, 1956. Quoted in: Benson, *Nelson Mandela, the Man and the Movement*, 61

Chapter 6
1. Winnie Mandela, *Part of My Soul Went with Him* (London: Victor Gollancz Ltd.; New York: W.W. Norton & Company, 1985): 57
2. Nancy Harrison, *Winnie Mandela* (London: Victor Gollancz Ltd. New York: George Braziller Publishers, 1985): 52

3. Mandela, *Part of My Soul Went with Him* 57-58
4. Ibid., 59
5. Harrison, *Winnie Mandela*, 63
6. Mandela, *No Easy Walk to Freedom*, 83-84

Chapter 7
1. Mandela, *No Easy Walk to Freedom*, 157
2. Benson, *Nelson Mandela, the Man and the Movement*, 101
3. Mandela, *No Easy Walk to Freedom*, 95
4. Mandela, *Part of My Soul Went with Him*, 73-74
5. Ibid., 75

Chapter 8
1. Mandela, *Part of My Soul Went with Him*, 76
2. Mandela, *No Easy Walk to Freedom*, 126
3. Ibid.
4. Ibid., 127
5. Ibid., 130
6. Ibid., 163
7. Mandela, *Part of My Soul Went with Him*, 82

Chapter 9
2. Harrison, *Winnie Mandela*, 106
2. Mandela, *Part of My Soul Went with Him*, 144
3. Benson, *Nelson Mandela, the Man and the Movement*, 234
4. Mandela, *Part of My Soul Went with Him*, 147-48

INDEX- *Page numbers in boldface type indicate illustrations.*

130

About the Author

Jim Hargrove has worked as a writer and editor for more than ten years. After serving as an editorial director for three Chicago area publishers, he began a career as an independent writer, preparing a series of books for children. He has contributed to works by nearly twenty different publishers. His Childrens Press titles include biographies of Mark Twain, Daniel Boone, Thomas Jefferson, Lyndon B. Johnson, Steven Spielberg, and Richard Nixon. With his wife and daughter, he lives in a small Illinois town near the Wisconsin border.